NILS
NAVARRO

ENDEMIC
BIRDS
OF CUBA

A COMPREHENSIVE
FIELD GUIDE

INCLUDING
WEST INDIAN ENDEMICS
RESIDING IN CUBA

EDICIONES NUEVOS MUNDOS
The Friendship Association

TEXT, ILLUSTRATIONS, AND PHOTOGRAPHY
Nils Navarro

ENGLISH EDITION
Soledad Pagliuca, Kathleen Hennessey,
Sharyn Thompson, and George Paidas

TRANSLATION
Loyda Sánchez

SCIENTIFIC CONSULTANT
James W. Wiley

DESIGN AND LAYOUT
Pepe Nieto

ADDITIONAL PHOTOGRAPHY
Ernesto Reyes, Juan Miguel Cruz,
Maikel Cañizares and Eladio Fernández

MAPS
Dagoberto Drigs and Nils Navarro

PUBLISHED BY
Ediciones Nuevos Mundos
www.EdicionesNuevosMundos.com

ISBN: 978-0-9909419-1-0
© 2015 Nils Navarro
© 2015 Ediciones Nuevos Mundos

PRINTED IN CHINA BY
Four Colour Print Group

To Betty Petersen,
a great friend and inspiration,
for her love of birds and her
dedication to their protection
and conservation.

To future generations,
confident that they will
continue to preserve our
heritage of biodiversity in
Cuba, the islands of the
Caribbean, and the entire
planet.

Contents

Acknowledgements

This book was made possible thanks to the encouragement and support offered by BirdLife International; British Birdwatching Fair; BirdsCaribbean (formerly The Society for the Conservation and Study of Caribbean Birds (SCSCB)); The Christopher Reynolds Foundation; the American Birding Association through the Birders' Exchange program (ABA-BEX); Rufford Small Grants Foundation; Optics for the Tropics; Caribbean Heritage Concepts; Eric Hosking Charitable Trust; Idea Wild; Wilderness Graphics; the Centro Nacional de Áreas Protegidas de Cuba (CNAP); and the Sociedad Cubana de Zoología.

In particular I wish to thank David Wege, Veronica Ánadon, Herbert Raffaelle, James W. Wiley, Lisa Sorenson, Joni Ellis, Lourdes Mujica, Betty Petersen (†), Jane Raymond, Rosemarie Gnan, Leo Douglas, Jennifer Wheeler, and Marvin and Lee Cook. My sincere thanks to Loyda Sánchez of Massachusetts Audubon Society, Panama, for accepting the challenge of producing an excellent English translation.

To my wonderful friends who shared their photographs for use in this publication and whose names appear in the credits, and to my colleagues who helped with the revision of the manuscript and with other aspects of the organization of the final product: Wayne Petersen, Susana Aguilar, Ramona Oviedo, Bárbara Sánchez, Hiram González, Arturo Kirkconnell, Orlando Garrido, Luis M. Díaz, Gilberto Silva Taboada, Carolina Gutiérrez, Maikel Cañizares, Freddy Rodríguez, Eduardo Iñigo, Wilf Simcox, Eneider Pérez, Sergio Colón, Alfred Roca, Margie Bauer, Martín Acosta, José Manuel Pantaleón (Cimarrón Mayor Panta).

To Eduardo Abreu, Omar Labrada, Gerardo Begué, Francisco Alcolea, and Alexis Silva, for their invaluable assistance in the field excursions, and to my inseparable friends Carlos Peña, Ernesto Reyes, Alejandro Fernández, Feliberto Bermúdez (Félix), Alfredo Rams, and Rubisnay Leyva. In particular, to Alejandro Torres (†), Rafael Abreu, and Jorge de la Cruz for opening the way to understanding the fauna of Cuba.

To Zoyla, Rogelio, Rosa, Edelis, Claudina, and Pedro, for their inestimable support, to Charles Duncan for his friendship, and for his help whenever possible, to Rafaela Aguilera for her support during the research of the bird collections of the Instituto de Ecología y Sistemática de Cuba (IES).

To Luke Mahller and the curators Nathan Rice of the Academy of Natural

Sciences of Philadelphia (ANSP); Joel L. Cracarft and Peter Capainolo of the American Museum of Natural History (AMNH); Eric Kershner and Christopher Milensky of the US National Museum of Natural History (USNMNH) for their help with access to reference material in their collections.

My gratitude to my dear friends Patricia Lancho and Juan Llamacho for their assistance and hospitality, and to Yvonne Árias, Kate Wallace, and Jorge Brocca for their help with research in the Dominican Republic.

To my dear friend Eladio Fernández, who personally contributed a substantial part of the photographic equipment utilized and gave me invaluable advice on nature photography, affording me the possibility of creating a sizeable data bank of images of Cuban and Caribbean birds. To Izuky Pérez, who offered his photography laboratory and technical support for copies of the original illustrations.

To Pépe Nieto for his excellent design and layout of the book, and for his wise and opportune suggestions. Indispensable were the editors Soledad Pagliuca, Kathleen Hennessey, and Sharyn Thompson, who believed in the importance of creating a work of exceptional quality, and who refused to accept anything less for the readers. To you, my friends, my eternal thanks for your involvement and dedication.

To my wife, Yerenia García Álvarez for being my inspiration. Without her unwavering support and dedication, it would never have been possible to complete this book. To my children, Alejandro, Noel, and Diego, three more reasons for persevering with this dream, and for Alejandro's participation in the creation of the digital images.

I could not conclude without thanking my father, Nils, my brother, Alberto, and especially my mother, Magalys Pacheco, for their concern, encouragement, and many sacrifices to help bring this work to fruition, and because I know how proud they will be when it is finally a reality for all.

Foreword

This book began with the idea of designing a pocket field guide to the endemic birds of Cuba, with basic texts and illustrations. Nevertheless, the experience of intense days of research in the parks and protected areas of Cuba, and speaking with biologists and technicians in the field who expressed their need for appropriate printed material for the identification of birds, brought me to reconsider the original concept.

The idea was expanded to include a combination of interests in conservation and recreation. A new concept emerged: an interactive field guide; not a computer-based program, but a book printed on paper, designed according to the practical needs of those who do field biology as well as for birdwatchers who simply find pleasure in the careful observation of nature. The book's design provides space for the user to add personal field notes about feeding habits, habitat, distribution, nesting, patterns of behavior, color and markings, and other remarks.

This field guide offers the reader up-to-date information, with illustrations that present the birds in various typical postures as well as in silhouettes for identification in conditions of poor visibility. Some birds have never been illustrated in this way before. Included are maps with indications of how and where to travel in Cuba; important sites for the observation of birds; identification of habitats; and criteria for management of endangered species. Without further explanation, you are invited to browse these pages with the hope that you will learn from this book, add to it, and even become a co-author. It will be a pleasure to work together!

Nils Navarro

Prologue

JAMES W. WILEY

Cuba, the largest island in the West Indies, lures scientists and naturalists with its geographical and biological diversity. Being an island, separated from mainland sources, Cuba exhibits a high level of endemism; many species of plants and animals evolved in isolation and are found nowhere else in the world. Sadly, among Cuba's 26 endemic bird species, 22 (85%) are of national and international concern because of fear for their continued survival.

Nils Navarro has a close personal relationship with his native Cuba and, especially, its natural environment. A well-respected scientist, Nils' investigations have taken him throughout most of the archipelago. In addition to his quest for scientific knowledge, Nils' explorations have been driven by his ambition to capture the beauty of his country and its natural resources for others to appreciate. Nils is an extraordinarily talented artist who is able to accurately translate his field observations into beautiful and diagnostic illustrations that provide the viewer with an appreciation of the majesty of his subjects.

Inspired by his deep personal concern for Cuba's declining bird populations, Nils has produced this comprehensive and unique field guide to Cuba's endemic birds, with the goal of increasing awareness of his country's birds and their environment. Each of the Cuban endemic accounts includes superb illustrations of birds in typical postures from different perspectives that provide characteristics for identifying the species, along with concise written cues for identification. In addition to these endemic species, Nils has included illustrations and characteristics for another 22 species that are endemic to the West Indies, and which include the Cuban Archipelago in their distribution.

The attraction of the guide is not restricted to scientists, naturalists, and casual birdwatchers because everyone can appreciate Nils' beautiful renderings of the exquisite feathered jewels of Cuba. Nils urges users of his guide to expand what he has provided by adding their own observations in the form of notes in spaces provided through the book. He encourages exploration of the islands through detailed maps and descriptions of habitats where the more restricted endemic birds might be found. Cuba retains large areas of original and moderately disturbed habitat, much of it under safeguard within the National System of Protected Areas. It is in these protected areas that many species unable to adapt to the changing landscape elsewhere have

A Night on the White Side (Bare-legged Owl, *Margarobyas lawrencii*). Watercolor on paper by Nils Navarro. Courtesy of Mary Linden

found refuge and where the user of this guide, searching for some of the rarer endemic birds, may be rewarded with discovery.

Nils' compassion for his native Cuba and concern for its ecosystem is obvious throughout the guide. His concern for Cuba's avifauna is extended to the readers as Nils encourages them to help in improving knowledge and conservation of the island's birds by contributing their sightings to appropriate archives of such information.

Through Nils' artistry and words, we can all better appreciate the natural treasures of Cuba.

Cuban Trogon
(*Priotellus temnurus*)

1
How to Use This Guide

What's in the field guide?

Practical information about 48 species of birds: 26 endemic to Cuba and another 22 that are endemic to the West Indies and which include the Cuban Archipelago in their distribution.

The guide synthesizes recently compiled information about bird identification, food, behavior, habitats, nesting, distribution, maps, threat of extinction status, and the current Cuban regulations concerning the environment and the protection of the flora and fauna. Space for field notes is also included.

The American Birding Association (ABA) (www.aba.org); *The Clements Checklist of Birds of the World,* 2013 (www.birds.cornell.edu/clementschecklist); and the American Ornithologists' Union (AOU), 2014 (www.aou.org) criteria were followed for the taxonomy and organization of species. However, differences of opinion by notable experts in the field were also taken into consideration.

How is the guide structured?

To quickly identify a bird in the field, consult the front and back covers for illustrations of the 26 endemic species of Cuba with their common name and the page number where a detailed description is located.

The back inside flap contains a key to all the symbols for the description of the endemic birds. Each chapter is distinguished by a different color covering the page number.

How to Use this Guide offers information on the structure of the book; the section **Getting to Know Cuba** provides an overview of the general geographical characteristics of the Cuban archipelago, including basic information on its biodiversity and bird population. A special section on **Frequently Asked Questions** addresses concerns about birding in Cuba.

In Chapter 2 you will find a description of the endemic birds of Cuba and those of the West Indies that reside in Cuba. **Endemic Birds of Cuba** contains descriptions and illustrations for each Cuban endemic, depicting the species from different angles and postures. Silhouettes will assist in the identification process when a bird is against the light or its colors are difficult to distinguish.

Colored boxes indicate the threat

of extinction status (if available) according to the International Union for Conservation of Nature (IUCN) and the *Libro Rojo de los Vertebrados Cubanos* (2012) (Red Data Book for Cuban Vertebrates). There is a space for noting the number of each birdcall recording, if available.

The following information corresponds to each species listed in the chapter on Cuban endemics:

1. **NAMES:** English name(s) according to the American Ornithological Union; Alpha code; scientific name in italics; local name(s) in Cuba; and standard name as accepted by the Sociedad Española de Ornitología (SEO).

2. **IDENTIFICATION:** Bird length (inches/cm), with a detailed description of the morphological and color characteristics, behavior patterns, and comments of interest. Comparisons between sexes appear only where dimorphism occurs.

3. **VOICE:** As much as possible, vocalizations are onomatopoetical.

4. **GEOGRAPHIC VARIATION:** Subspecies are listed and referred to on the plate corresponding to each species, both for the illustrations and the distribution map. Other patterns of geographic variation are presented when evident.

5. **SIMILAR SPECIES:** The bird is compared to other species with which it might be confused in the field.

6. **STATUS, DISTRIBUTION, AND HABITAT:** Current data is provided on the level of threat to the species, on geographic distribution, and details about habitats, with icons that illustrate each of the three categories.

7. **FEEDING:** The bird's diet is described, including its major food components. Feeding behavior is noted if it is an important feature for identification. Icons can be modified to add information.

8. **NESTING:** Information is given on the time of year the bird breeds, followed by the location, characteristics, and construction material for the nest, and the number, size, color, and shape of the eggs.

9. **REFERENCE LOCALITIES:** Known and easily accessible sites are listed, with their general region noted (western **W**, central **C** and eastern **E** Cuba), as well as the province to which they belong.

PROVINCE	CODE
Artemisa	**Ar**
Camagüey	**Cm**
Ciego de Ávila	**CA**
Cienfuegos	**Cf**
Granma	**Gr**
Guantánamo	**Gt**
Holguín	**Ho**
Isla de la Juventud	**IJ**
Havana	**Hb**
Las Tunas	**LT**
Matanzas	**Mt**
Mayabeque	**Mb**
Pinar del Río	**PR**
Sancti Spíritus	**SS**
Santiago de Cuba	**SC**
Villa Clara	**VC**

The section **West Indian Endemic Birds Residing in Cuba** illustrates regional endemic birds and discusses their level of threat, geographic distribution, and habitat in an abbreviated way.

Birds in their Habitats describes the

Cuban Green Woodpecker (*Xiphidiopicus percussus*)

general characteristics of different vegetation formations with a qualitative reference to measure the richness of bird species in each habitat, and indicates the presence of the most frequently encountered endemics. Photographs of the main habitats are included, as well as photographs of the endemic and regionally endemic birds in their habitats.

Conservation Status of Threatened Birds offers information on the level of threat of Cuban and West Indian endemics residing in Cuba, according to BirdLife International (2014) and the Red Data Book, followed by current Cuban laws on conservation.

A detailed selection of **Maps** shows topography, political-administrative divisions, roads, localities referenced in the guide, parks, protected areas, main cities, hotels, airports, and service points for gasoline and food.

At the end of the field guide are the indices for **Localities and Species**. Space is provided for personal notes and for recording anecdotal observations for future reference. There is a page to record contacts with local guides, ornithologists, colleagues and other persons and institutions, as well as a calendar to note dates of the first appearance of nests and eggs, migration, etc. A **Checklist of Cuban and Other West Indian Endemic Birds Residing in the Cuban Archipelago** will help with important sightings, which should be reported to EBIRD (www.ebird.org) and other institutions involved in conservation and documentation. Remember to use a waterproof marker or a 5B pencil!

Getting to Know Cuba

General Characteristics

Cuba, one of the island groups comprising the Greater Antilles, is the largest island in the West Indies. It forms an archipelago of 42,829 sq. miles (110,926 km²) dominated by two main islands: Cuba, with 40,543 sq. miles (105,007 km²), and Isla de la Juventud (Isle of Youth), with 851 sq. miles (2,204 km²). They are surrounded by more than 4,195 islands, islets, and cays, in four archipelagos: Los Colorados, Sabana-Camagüey (Jardines del Rey), Jardines de la Reina, and Los Canarreos.

Cuba is approximately 776 miles (1,250 km) long by 118 miles (191 km) at its widest point. It is surrounded by deep basins in the Caribbean Sea, the Gulf of Mexico, and the Florida and Bahama Straits. These basins are the true geographic limits of the Republic of Cuba. The country is divided into 15 provinces and one special municipality: Isla de la Juventud. The population is over 11 million inhabitants and the official language is Spanish. Mountains occupy 18% of the national territory and are distributed in three main, geographically separated groups: western, central, and eastern regions. Elevations found in Cuba are classified as:

• Premontane: 984-1,639 feet (300-499 meters)
• Small mountains: 1,640-3,279 feet (500-999 meters)
• Low mountains: 3,280-4,919 feet (1,000-1,499 meters)
• Mountains: >4,920 feet (>1,500 meters)

The highest peaks are: Pico Turquino in the Sierra Maestra at 6,476 feet (1,974 meters); Pico Cristal in the Nipe-Sagua-Baracoa mountains at

Sagua-Baracoa Sierra, eastern part of Cuba

4,039 feet (1,231 meters); Pico San Juan in the Guamuhaya range of central Cuba at 3,740 feet (1,140 meters); and Pan de Guajaibón in the Cordillera de Guaniguanico at 2,195 feet (699 meters). Extensive low plains, representing 75% of the territory, separate these mountain groups.

Cuban rivers are short and relatively shallow. The Toa River has the greatest volume, while the Cauto River is the longest.

Coastal wetlands support a high richness of water birds. Mangroves have a special significance for protection, stability, and biological productivity of coastal zones, covering 4.8% of Cuba's surface, and representing 26% of the country's forest cover.

Cuba has a moderate, subtropical climate, which is strongly influenced by trade winds. Two main seasons occur: dry (November-April) and rainy (May-October), with similar duration and temperatures. The average annual temperature is 74.5°F (23.5°C): 71.6°F (22°C) during the dry season when Cuba receives cold air masses from the north, and 77°F (25°C) during the rainy season. The average relative humidity is 80%.

The annual precipitation is approximately 54" (1,374 mm). The lowest accumulations occur in the southeastern part of Cuba, notably Guantánamo, with 8"-23.5" (200-600 mm) annually. The highest values are also in the province of Guantánamo, in the eastern mountains, and range from 63" to over 134" (1,600 mm-3,400 mm). In recent years, the precipitation rate throughout Cuba has decreased, causing exceptionally dry periods and droughts.

Biodiversity and Endemism

Cuba is known for its biological diversity. The island has a great variety of ecosystems and landscapes, richness of species, and a high number of endemics at the local and provincial levels.

A species is considered endemic when it inhabits a single location, region,

Cuban land snail (*Polymita picta*)

Blind fish (*Lucifuga dentata*)

or country and is not found outside its range. Some individuals may be circumstantially erratic or arbitrarily or accidentally introduced to some other place; this does not exempt the species from the category of endemic.

Cuba's high endemism is due in part to its geographical isolation and the proximity of continental and island land masses that have continually shared flora and fauna. Add to this the complex geomorphological and paleogeographical structure of the territory and the diversity of types of rock and soil, factors that have generated a high diversity of habitats. Other important factors are the altitudinal and climatic differences. The study of an endemic species that is unique to a particular place or region is invaluable for the conservation of biodiversity, and contributes important biogeographic indicators that help scientists to model theories on the origin, growth, and evolution of species. These endemic plants and animals should take priority in conservation programs. Being restricted to certain areas makes them vulnerable to extinction, both from anthropogenic and natural causes. Endemism at both the island and the local level is mostly found in mountainous zones and swamps. Many of these habitats have limited extention and are prone to deforestation and alteration.

Cuba has no dangerous or highly poisonous animals, which makes the archipelago a paradise that houses the greatest biodiversity in the Antilles. The biota includes approximately 32,080 species of plants and animals. Of these, 6,500 species are vascular plants with endemism higher than 50%, two percent of which are threatened

Monte Iberia frog (*Eleutherodactylus iberia*)

to some degree. Over 400 species of orchids are among the most attractive plants because of the beautiful colors and shapes of their flowers.

Cuban fauna includes 16,553 known species. Invertebrates are the least known; estimates are that about half are yet to be described. Land vertebrates are much better known, with 62 species of amphibians (95% endemic), 57 species of freshwater fish (37% endemic), 155 reptiles (79% endemic), 371 birds (7.7% endemic), and 52 mammals (32% endemic). Cuban fauna boasts some of the smallest animals on earth, such as the tiny Cuban scorpion (*Microtityus fundorai*), about ½ inch (13 mm) in length; the Monte Iberia frog (*Eleutherodactylus iberia*) about ⅓ inch long (8.3 mm); the Bee Hummingbird (*Mellisuga helenae*), 2½ inches (63 mm); and Gervais's funnel-eared bat (*Nyctiellus lepidus*), weighing only 0.10 ounces (3 grams). Though not the smallest snail, the colorful Polymita is one of Cuba's natural gems.

Gervais's funnel-eared bat (*Nyctiellus lepidus*)

© ELADIO FERNANDEZ

Cuban Avifauna

Birds possess the highest diversity of terrestrial vertebrates in Cuba. Currently 371 species have been described, belonging to 21 orders, 67 families (one of which, Teretistridae, is endemic) and 218 genera, seven of which are endemic (*Cyanolimnas,*

Bee Hummingbird (*Mellisuga helenae*)

Starnoenas, Margarobyas, Xiphidiopicus, Ferminia, Teretistris, and *Torreornis*). Remarkably, 62% of the bird species in the West Indies occur in Cuba. Among these, 285 are residents or regular visitors, 42% nest in the archipelago, and 70% are migratory. Endemism is 7.7%, with 26 endemic species currently recognized. The Cuban Macaw (*Ara tricolor*) is the only endemic bird to become extinct in recent times; the last official report was in 1864. Some Cuban endemics, such as the Cuban Kite, Zapata Wren, Zapata Rail, and Cuban Sparrow (Zapata Sparrow), occur only at very

limited sites. The Sparrow's distribution is disjointed.

One species that has become an icon for conservationists is the Ivory-billed Woodpecker. Its current status is highly controversial, but a few individual birds may still exist in the eastern mountains of the island. Nevertheless, the risk of its extinction is extremely high. Curiosities such as the Bee Hummingbird, considered the smallest bird in the world, and other colorful birds (Cuban Trogon, Cuban Tody, and Cuban Parrot), and those with superb songs (Cuban Solitaire, Zapata Wren, Cuban Gnatcatcher, and Cuban Grassquit) characterize the Cuban avifauna.

There are two well-defined groups among migratory birds. One includes the winter resident species that reach Cuba during the fall migration from North America. This is the larger group and includes a great variety of birds such as ducks, gulls, warblers, sparrows, and shorebirds. The fall migration occurs mainly from August through October, although some species arrive as early as mid-July, whereas others that breed in North America may arrive as late as November.

The spring migration for arriving or returning migrants begins in late February when many species congregate on the coasts to await favorable weather conditions. This reaches a peak in April and ends in May. The main migratory bird corridors in Cuba are: Guanahacabibes in Pinar del Río province; Cárdenas in Matanzas province; Santa Fé in La Habana province; Cayería Norte de

Bare-legged Owl nest
(*Margarobyas lawrencii*)

Cuban Tody nest
(*Todus multicolor*)

Cuban Green Woodpecker nest
(*Xiphidiopicus percussus*)

Camagüey in the province of Ciego de Ávila; and Gibara in Holguín.

The second migratory group, the summer residents, includes 14 species arriving from South America, mainly in March. Among the most common are the Gray Kingbird, Antillean Nighthawk, Black-whiskered Vireo, Cuban Martin, and Wilson's Plover. All breed in Cuba and leave in September through October.

Nesting

The breeding period for the endemic birds discussed here is variable according to the species, but occurs primarily between March and July. The structure and location of the nest are also variable. In many cases interdependent relationships are established among nesting species because of limited habitat or nest-construction abilities. Woodpeckers, for instance, excavate cavities in tree trunks that are later used by other birds such as the Cuban Pygmy Owl, Bare-legged Owl, Cuban Parakeet, Rose-throated Parrot, and Cuban Trogon, none of which creates its own nest. The Cuban Tody excavates holes in mounds of earth and rotten tree stumps. Other species use plant and animal fibers to construct their nests. In general, knowing the way in which each species makes its nest is an effective tool for detecting its presence.

Red-legged Thrush nest (*Turdus plumbeus*)

Cuban Nightjar nest (*Antrostomus cubanensis*)

Subspecies and geographical variations

Subspecies constitute populations that belong to the same species and present moderate but consistent variations in color, size, and/or behavior and has resulted in geographical variations in some bird species, with a tendency toward larger size and increased color intensity in a gradient extending from the cays and coasts into the mountains.

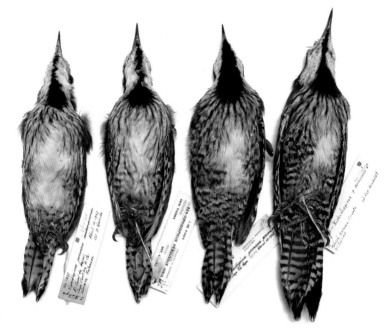

Some species exhibit variations in color and size within the Cuban archipelago. The Cuban Green Woodpecker (*Xiphidiopicus percussus*) populations differ from the coast and the cays (left), to mountainous areas (right).

ecology, although these differences are quite often not discernible in the field. Furthermore, populations designated as subspecies may occur in different areas. At times these subspecies may overlap and breed among themselves. Cuba's vast ecological landscape varies from extremely dry coastal environments to zones of high humidity in the mountains. In addition, its great geological diversity makes Cuba an archipelago with heterogeneous characteristics. This

Certain variations have been interpreted as subspecific differences, notably the Cuban Green Woodpecker, West Indian Woodpecker, Cuban Pewee, Cuban Vireo, Great Lizard-Cuckoo, Loggerhead Kingbird, and Cuban Trogon. Described diagnostic parameters used to distinguish populations, however, can be weak arguments for separation at the subspecific level; therefore, some populations are treated as geographical variations in this guidebook.

Threats

Birds, like all plant and animal species, are continually exposed to natural disasters and human-generated stress. Natural disasters, such as large, out-of-control fires, excessive rains, and droughts are a threat to animal species and their habitats. Hurricanes can create severe damage to the natural ecosystem causing the loss of habitat, food, and nesting sites over long periods of time. Human-generated threats in Cuba include: habitat destruction as a consequence of urbanization, development of the sugar industry, tourism, and mining. Habitat loss accelerated at the height of the "special period" (1990s), when the lack of fuel on the island resulted in an intensified and uncontrolled felling of trees.

Painted Bunting, Indigo Bunting, and Rose-breasted Grosbeak. People involved in this activity are known as *pajareros*, and they are especially active in Santa Fé (Havana province) and Gibara (Holguín province). This tradition is consequential in increasing

Typical *pajarero* working the illegal bird trade

The invasive African sharptooth catfish (*Clarias gariepinus*) is one of the primary threats to freshwater Cuban fauna.

Hunting is a sport regulated by the Cuban Federation of Sport Hunting and is not considered a threat to conservation; poaching, however, is a problem for certain medium-size species, especially ducks and pigeons. Capturing songbirds for the wildlife trade poses a threat to the survival of species such as the Cuban Grassquit, Yellow-faced Grassquit, Cuban Bullfinch, Western Spindalis, Rose-throated Parrot, Cuban Parakeet,

the illegal national and international trafficking of wild birds, which has resulted in a substantial decrease in their populations.

The introduction of exotic and invasive species such as cats, dogs, pigs, mongooses, and the African sharptooth catfish (*Clarias gariepinus*) has caused unavoidable impacts on the native fauna. The recently introduced catfish has the ability to slither across land and consume large numbers of eggs, young, and even adults, making it one of the main threats to birds associated with bodies of fresh water.

Damaged coastal area in Holguin province after Hurricane Ike (2008)

Pollution generated by industrial processes, as well as the intensive use of pesticides in agriculture, combine to quickly destroy entire food chains in rivers, lagoons, and other ecosystems. Presently, eight percent of Cuban bird species are considered by BirdLife International to be in one of the five categories of threat; of these, 47% are endemic species. An additional 63% are endemics of the Caribbean area. The Red Data Book lists 30 threatened species and two near threatened, a total of 8.7% of registered Cuban birds. If you observe any threatened species, please report the location to the local authorities of the Ministry of Science, Technology, and Environment (CITMA), Park welcome centers, protected areas, museums, or other appropriate institutions.

Conservation

Cuba has a National System of Protected Areas (Sistema Nacional de Áreas Protegidas)(SNAP) that prioritizes the *in situ* conservation of biological diversity. In total, 22% of the national territory is within the

SNAP, which incorporates areas of local significance. These include a broad mosaic of small reserves as well as extensive zones in mountain ranges and other areas. There are a total of 91 areas of national importance and 162 areas of local importance. The administration of each area develops

Conservation efforts in protected areas: creating artificial nests for parrots and parakeets

Community event "Protecting Birds" held in Gibara. A Caribbean Endemic Bird Festival sponsored by BirdsCaribbean

prioritized conservation programs for threatened and endemic species and for other relevant populations. The Important Bird Area (IBA) program of BirdLife International was established in Cuba in 2000. A total of 28 IBAs are recognized, covering 18% of Cuba; more than 80% are in the National Protected Areas. The most critical sites are Ciénaga de Zapata and Humboldt National Park.

Each year, from April 22 to May 22, BirdsCaribbean organizes the "Caribbean Endemic Bird Festival" at the regional level that has substantially contributed to promoting conservation of endemic birds. This festival is a model of how everyone can participate in the preservation of Cuban avifauna by organizing local birdwatching groups, art contests for children, community workshops, poster exhibitions, and developing promotional materials with messages designed to encourage bird conservation.

Cuban Parakeet (*Psittacara euops*): monitoring and banding fledglings around the nesting areas of the Cauto river basin

Birdwatching in Cuba: FAQs

Where can a visiting birdwatcher go in Cuba?

There are numerous sites for birdwatching in Cuba, many of them in public zones of the protected areas (see **Maps** section) that provide local guide services and other facilities. Cuba is a country with a rich history and culture, and friendly, hospitable people. Two weeks on the island are usually sufficient for a birdwatcher to visit the most important birding areas and also enjoy Cuba's music, museums, art, and beaches.

The success of a birdwatching trip depends, to a great extent, on the assistance of a qualified and knowledgeable guide. Beware of people pretending to be experts in the field. Several travel agencies offer programs that include visits to places with optimum potential for birdwatching with experienced guides.

Throughout Cuba, but especially in the provincial capitals, car rental agencies offer a variety of vehicle types. A typical birdwatching route will not exceed 1,200 miles (2,000) km.

Essential birdwatching sites:

1. Viñales, Las Terrazas, San Diego de los Baños, La Güira, and Soroa, in the western part of Cuba. Important for special Cuban endemics like the Cuban Solitaire, Cuban Grassquit, and Oriente Warbler, as well as for offering some of the most beautiful landscapes in the country.

2. Zapata Peninsula (Playa Larga, Bermejas, Pálpite, La Turba, Las Salinas, and Hatiguanico) is the largest wetland in the Caribbean and is considered to be the most important region for birdwatching in Cuba.

3. Cayo Coco, Cayo Paredón Grande, and Cayo Guillermo, in the group of

Las Salinas, in Ciénaga de Zapata, an important shorebird observation site

cays north of central Cuba where there are extensive low-lying marshy areas with an abundance of aquatic birds. One can observe the Cuban endemics and near endemics: Cuban Sparrow, Cuban Gnatcatcher, Thick-billed Vireo, and the Bahama Mockingbird.

4. Sierra de Najasa, Sierra de Cubitas, and Río Máximo in Camagüey Province. Excellent areas for observing species such as the Cuban Parakeet, Giant Kingbird, Palm Crow, Plain Pigeon, and the largest colony of nesting Flamingos in the Caribbean.

5. Parque Nacional Alejandro de Humboldt. Situated in the eastern mountainous areas of Cuba, the park's pristine forests are the last refuge of the critically endangered Cuban Kite and where the Ivory-billed Woodpecker was last spotted.

When is the best time of year for birdwatching?
Between January and April: temperatures are comfortable, days are not too sunny, and rain is infrequent. October and November are also good for birding because of the presence of many migratory birds. Keep in mind that hurricane season extends from June through the end of November. July and August are the hottest months, with frequent storms and fewer birds.

What is the best time of day for birdwatching?
One to four hours after dawn. Hours close to midday are good mostly for locating nesting birds and for observing shorebirds. Around sundown is good for sighting crepuscular and night birds. Night observation will reveal the Bare-legged Owl, the Screech Owl, and the Cuban Nightjar.

What are the most favorable weather conditions for birdwatching?
Bird activity will vary depending on weather conditions. Wind, rain, cold fronts, and high or low temperatures influence bird behavior. The days following rainy and cool periods are especially recommended for birdwatching, when the morning is warm, sunny, clear, and calm.

What should I wear on the field trip?
Remember that Cuba has a warm climate! An appropriate wardrobe for birdwatching would be waterproof boots, a long-sleeved shirt (to avoid mosquito bites and scratches), lightweight, long pants of durable material, and a cap or hat for protection from the sun. All of these clothes should be in muted tones of green, gray, and tan.
During the "winter" months (December through February), temperatures may become relatively cool, which, combined with high humidity, accentuates the feeling of cold. It is advisable to bring a light jacket, especially for mountainous zones.

What should I bring on the outing?
Above all, don't forget to bring this guidebook! Also bring binoculars, and a waterproof pen. Maximum temperatures are in July and August; however, at any time of the year be sure to bring sunscreen, water, and some nutritional snacks.

Raingear is recommended, as are waterproof bags to protect equipment and field guides from humidity and rain, especially during the rainy season. When visiting areas close to coasts or swamps, remember to bring insect repellent. Mosquitoes and biting midges ("no-see-ums") abound in these areas, and are usually most annoying after rainy periods in the summer, early in the morning, and at dusk.

What are the guidelines for a successful birdwatching excursion?

Be sure to have binoculars handy when approaching the site. Be silent or speak softly. Initially, stay for a brief time observing and listening to everything around you; this will allow for quick adaptation to the environment. Walk slowly and carefully. Avoid sudden movements and stop for observation frequently. Most birds perch above chest level. However, some, such as terrestrial pigeons and grassland or thicket-dwelling birds, will be closer to the ground. Avoid pointing at a bird with an extended arm; rather, just flex your arm on your chest and point with your finger.

What about birdcalls?

Judicious use of sound recordings is acceptable under certain circumstances. Do not abuse this technique. To avoid creating unnecessary disturbances and stress on the birds, never use birdcalls during breeding or nesting seasons.

How can I find many species in a short time?

Endemic birds are often found together in various habitats. Knowing such associations will minimize search time and effort. The table on the next page shows which groups of species are commonly associated (first group as reference to match the others).

What photographic equipment should I bring?

A camera is not necessary to effectively observe birds in their natural habitat. However, among birdwatchers worldwide, photography has become very popular.

A compact camera or cell phone can give good results. For the more serious photographer, the suggested equipment is a digital single lens reflex camera and a 70-300 mm interchangeable zoom lens with auto focus and, preferably, with image-stabilization (IS/VR) technology or similar. Use a remote-control shooting device and a light tripod or monopod if possible. If you are using a spotting scope, you may be able to shoot directly through the scope. This may require a coupling device.

A 100-400 ISO will yield good results because Cuban light is very intense. Remember that in elevated ISOs, images may look granulated and less sharp. Program the camera to high resolution for the best quality photographs; this will take up more space on your memory card.

Use battery chargers with AC/DC adapters and bring several batteries charged in advance (Cuba uses standard 110 V). Bring several cards of 8 GB each; in the event of loss or malfunction, only a small part of the photographs will be lost. The use of a portable mini hard drive for

SPECIES		ASOCIATION	CONDITIONS
Cuban Tody			
Cuban Vireo			
Oriente Warbler			Regional Endemics (Eastern)
Yellow-headed Warbler			Regional Endemics (Western)
Cuban Green Woodpecker			Very cryptic
Cuban Pygmy Owl			Very cryptic
Cuban Nightjar			Very cryptic
Cuban Trogon			Shady, humid areas
Bare-legged Owl			
Cuban Oriole			
Gray-fronted Quail-Dove			Patchy distribution
Blue-headed Quail-Dove			Patchy distribution
Bee Hummingbird			Patchy distribution
Cuban Solitaire			Patchy distribution
Gundlach's Hawk			Patchy distribution

■■■ VERY HIGH　　　■■■ HIGH　　　▨▨▨ MEDIUM

downloads can be very useful when in the field for several days.

Coastal environments have a high level of salinity. In the mountains, the relative humidity is very high, and during the early morning hours considerable moisture may condense on lens surfaces. After each session clean your equipment carefully. Bring cleaning accessories and protective bags for all camera equipment. Small silica gel bags are useful to reduce humidity inside transportation covers. With digital SLR cameras, avoid changing the lens frequently in the field to reduce the chance of dust entering the sensor.

Finally, be extra patient!

Can I use a flash?
Some professional birdwatchers prohibit the use of a flash especially during the breeding and nesting season because of the potential stress to the birds. Remember that a flash often overexposes the photograph, affects natural colors, and creates undesirable reflections and shadows on the animal or other close objects. The flash is not recommended when photographing birds with iridescent plumage, such as hummingbirds, trogons, todies, parakeets, and parrots.

How does a bird indicate it has been disturbed?
It is difficult to know how close a

bird will allow a person to approach, because every species differs in its behavioral pattern. Taking into account the observer is "invading" the bird's space, the birdwatcher should always keep in mind ethical rules to minimize the stress caused to the species or adjacent populations. Disturbances

Territorial display of the Killdeer (*Charadrius vociferus*)

while birds are feeding, foraging, nesting, or simply resting may have fateful consequences, especially if the effect is cumulative. Birds are then exposed to disruptions that cause them to flee far from their nest, which can result in sudden temperature changes in the eggs, and exposure of hatchlings to predators.

Look for very obvious behavior patterns of disturbance, such as:
• The bird stops feeding
• It looks in your direction
• It appears aggressive
• It is fluttering around
• It droops one wing as if injured
• It lifts its tail or head suddenly
• The colony mobs the intruder
These are signs of distress; move away immediately! Use binoculars or a spotting scope to get a better view.

Should I worry about diseases and poisonous plants?

Malaria, yellow fever, and other diseases associated with the tropics have been eradicated from Cuba. There is an occasional outbreak of dengue fever or cholera; however, the health department maintains strict controls and uses precautionary measures to prevent the spread of these diseases.

There are no animals in Cuba whose poison or bite is potentially lethal for humans. However, there are several plant species, some of them abundant, that may cause irritation, burns, or other skin problems by contact with their sap, thorns, or spiny hairs. It's a good idea to learn to identify these species.

Code of Birding Ethics
(From the American Birding Association guidelines)

Protecting the welfare of birds
- Respect the birds' territory, do not approach too closely
- Bird quietly, walk slowly, drive cautiously
- Be extra cautious around nests
- Never use audio playback near nesting areas
- Never use audio playback to attract threatened or endangered species
- Use audio playback sparingly, never in heavily birded areas
- Do not attract birds to dangerous areas (roads, areas with predators, unsanitary feeders and baths)
- Use flash sparingly when photographing birds
- The birds' welfare is the highest priority
- Do not harass birds by flushing, repeated calling, or shining spotlights
- Report your sightings to appropriate organizations
- Report rarities to appropriate organizations, but not necessarily to the general public if that would put the bird at risk

- Report poaching or other illegal activities to the authorities

Protecting habitat
- Do not damage habitat (litter, breaking branches, trampling vegetation)
- Stay on established paths and roads

Respecting the rights of others
- Respect private property
- Avoid aiming optics at people/homes
- Be a birding ambassador, promoting good relations with non-birders and the general public
- Follow the rules/regulations of public areas

Birding in groups
- Keep groups small
- The group leader is the only one to use "pishing" sounds.
- The group leader is responsible for the behavior of the group
- Be aware of others in your group and how your actions affect their enjoyment

Plants to avoid

Guao de costa (*Metopium toxiferum, M. brownei*): An arboreal plant that is abundant in coastal zones. It is distinguished by its ochre-colored trunk; thin, scaly bark with brown and black spots and an oily appearance.

Guao de peladero (*Metopium venosum*): Shrub or small tree that exists on serpentine rock formations in arid areas and pine forests in the northeastern part of Cuba. It is recognized by its shiny leaves and reddish color of the young shoots.

Guao de monte (*Comocladia dentata, C. platyphylla*): A shrubby plant with a thin, tall trunk; leaves are concentrated at the top. The leaves are deep green with a shiny surface and strongly serrated edges. This plant is common in open areas and secondary forests. The

Guao de monte (*Comocladia platyphylla*)

Guao de costa (*Metopium toxiferum*)

Guao de monte (*Comocladia dentata*)

Palo bronco (*Malpighia* spp.):
A small shrub with a thin, tall,
woody trunk, elongated leaves with
abundant spines, and deep red,
cherry-like fruits. It is common in
all forests and savannas throughout
Cuba and the Isla de la Juventud.
Its spines may adhere to the skin
or clothes, causing considerable
discomfort.

caustic latex from the three species of
Guao (pronounced gWOW!) produces
a strong irritation to the skin starting
with itching and dark brown spots that
cause inflamation and burns. People
with increased sensitivity to these
plants can suffer an allergic reaction
from simply standing under or near
the plant.

Palo bronco (*Malpighia* spp.)

Pringamosa (*Urera baccifera*)

Chichicate or Pringamosa (*Urera baccifera*): A shrubby plant with stems covered with thorns, and deep green, rounded broad leaves, with spiny protuberances on the leaf surface, abundant and rigid on the underside. Common in limestone elevations. Highly irritating.

Jazmín del pinar, Manzanillo (*Euphorbia podocarpifolia, E. helenae, E. muñisi*): Low and medium height

bush with gray trunk and large, deep green leaves. Tiny yellow flowers form in conspicuous red bracts. Common in bushy vegetation on serpentine rock in eastern Cuba. Its latex can generate burns from contact with the skin, and can cause diarrhea if accidentally swallowed.

Ortiguillas or Ortigas (*Fleurya* spp., *Platigyne* spp.): Climbing plants with small, finely spined leaves, found in

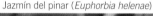

Jazmín del pinar (*Euphorbia helenae*)

association with other plants. It is common in forests and savannas. Ortiguilla produces a strong itching and mild local irritation, similar to ant bites, that gradually disappears. Avoid scratching.

Plants such as sawgrass ("cortadera," *Cladium jamaicense*) have jagged edges that can cause injuries to the skin. Sawgrass is common in the Ciénaga de Zapata. The pajúa palm (*Bactrix cubensis*) grows in mountainous areas; its trunk is covered with long spines that can easily puncture the skin when touched.

Ortiguilla (*Fleurya* sp.)

There is an extensive network of health services everywhere on the island; even in the mountains there are clinics, hospitals, and polyclinics. In the event of dermatological eruptions or cuts, it is always advisable to consult a doctor.

Palma pajúa (*Bactrix cubensis*)

Topography of a Bird

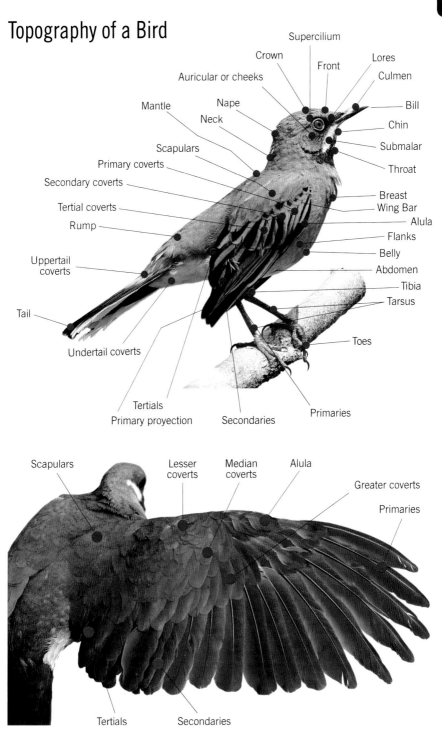

Gundlach's Hawk
(*Accipiter gundlachi*)

2

Endemic Birds of Cuba and the West Indies

IUCN
CR

Cuban Kite (CUKI)
Chondrohierax wilsonii
(formerly Hook-billed Kite, HBKI,
Chondrohierax uncinatus)
Gavilán Caguarero, Gavilán Sonso,
Gavilán Babosero, Gavilán Jabao,
Milano Caguarero (SEO)

IDENTIFICATION: 15"-17" (38-43 cm).
Sexes different. A robust raptor with
a large, elongated, hooked yellow bill
inclining to bluish at base. *Male:* Ashy-
gray upperparts, paler on the head.
Chest barred gray sometimes with
a ferruginous tinge. *Female:* Brown
upperparts and paler head, chest and
flanks marked with reddish-brown
bars on a white, cream or light tan
background, nuchal collar with white
background and barred. Both sexes
with indigo blue cere and bluish-white
iris. Wings broad and rounded, barred
beneath. Tail long, with three dark
bands below. Legs yellow-orange.
Juvenile: Very dark brown with ashy
zones on the upperparts, breast white
and finely or irregularly barred.
Occurs in pairs throughout the year.
A relatively tame bird, which many
farmers kill mistaking it for other
raptors that prey on their poultry. Like
other Kites, they soar on early morning
thermals. Soars and glides usually just
above treetops.
Considered by many ornithologists
as a subspecies of *C. uncinatus*; but
recently raised to the level of species,
currently validated on the basis of
comparative genetic and morphological
characteristics.

♂

♀

VOICE: Unknown. In similar species the call is a distinctive rattling, similar to pronouncing words, uttered when the bird is disturbed near its nest and during courtship.

SIMILAR SPECIES: The Broad-winged Hawk has a shorter tail, pointed wings without notable bands; bill is much smaller and the barred underparts do not reach the throat.

STATUS, DISTRIBUTION, AND HABITATS: The rarest of the Cuban raptors. Originally occurred throughout the island: **W Mt:** Ciénaga de Zapata, Ensenada de Cochinos (Bay of Pigs); **E Gr:** Río Cauto; **Ho:** Nuevo Mundo, Silla de Gibara; **Gt:** Guantánamo Bay, Boca de Jaibo, Monte Verde, Yateras. At present it has almost disappeared from the entire island, with reports only from the extreme east: **Gt:** Tribilín, Los Lirios, El Zapote.

FEEDING: Land snails (*Zachrysia, Polymita, Caracolus, Polydonte*). Usually feeds on the ground.

NESTING: Unknown.

NOTES

Gundlach's Hawk (GUHA)

Accipiter gundlachi
Gavilán Colilargo, Guaraguao,
Gavilán Rabilargo, Galilla,
Gavilán Cubano (SEO)

IDENTIFICATION: 17"-20" (43-51 cm). Elongated appearance. Tail long and rounded with brown bands. Wings long and rounded. Adult upperparts bluish to lead-gray and dull, with darker crown of the same color. Ventral parts barred reddish horizontally and gray toward the chest. Bill dark gray, darker close to the base. In flight a white patch on each side of the base of the tail is evident. *Male:* Smaller than female, which is duller in coloration. *Juvenile:* Dark brown above and streaked vertically with brown below.

VOICE: *Kec kec kec kec kec*, strong, somewhat nasal and shrill. During the breeding season it gives softer calls combined with a whistle repeated several times.

GEOGRAPHIC VARIATION: *A. g. gundlachi* (W) and *A. g. wileyi* (E). The populations are very similar.

SIMILAR SPECIES: The Sharp-shinned Hawk is much smaller and the tail tip is square rather than rounded, as in Gundlach's Hawk. The female Northern Harrier has a white rump. The Broad-winged Hawk is smaller with a stouter, robust body; its tail is shorter and plumage more heavily barred below.

STATUS, DISTRIBUTION, AND HABITATS: Rare, more frequent in the east. Distributed throughout Cuba and

Juv.

some cays to the north of Ciego de Ávila. Occurs in interior forests from sea level to elevations below 3,000 feet (900 meters), rural areas, swamps, and mangroves.

FEEDING: Carnivorous. Feeds on medium-sized birds such as parrots, gallinules, and pigeons; sometimes catches prey while perched on the ground.

NESTING: March-June, occasionally as early as late January. Nest, built with branches and twigs, and lined with grass, is below the canopy between 20 feet and 65 feet (7-20 meters), creating a crude platform supported by strong branches of tall trees. *Eggs:* 2-4, grayish-white or pale bluish-green.

REFERENCE LOCALITIES:

W PR: Guanahacabibes, Cabo San Antonio, Viñales, Sierra del Rosario, San Andres; **Mt:** Ciénaga de Zapata, Bermejas, La Turba; **Cf:** Laguna de Guanaroca, Casilda. **C CA:** Cayo Coco; **Cm:** Najasa, Sierra de Cubitas. **E Ho:** Gibara, Cupeycillo, El Embarcadero, Silla de Gibara, San Andrés, Cerros de Maniabón (Los Tibes); **SC:** El Cojo, Sierra Maestra

NOTES

Accipitridae

Cuban Black Hawk (CBHA)
Buteogallus gundlachii
Gavilán Batista, Copete,
Gavilán Cangrejero,
Buzardo Negro Norteño (SEO)

IDENTIFICATION: 20"-23" (51-58 cm).
Overall dark chocolate brown
with feathers edged light brown or
cinnamon, especially on the chest.
White patch on underside of wings.
Undertail coverts edged white. Flanks
with inconspicuous whitish bars. Tail
short with alternate white and dark
bands. Bill, cere, and legs yellow-
orange. In flight its broad and rounded
wings are notable. *Juvenile:* Lighter
brown with random white spots over
the whole body. Ventral parts usually
white with darker brown spots toward
the breast. Throat white and flanks
clearly striped with brown. Soars for
long periods. Recent studies support its
specific separation from the Common
Black-Hawk (*Buteogallus anthracinus*),
on the basis of morphological
characteristics and differences in
vocalization.

VOCALIZATION: Whistle-like call that
seems to pronounce the word *ba-tis-ta.*

SIMILAR SPECIES: Adults might be
mistaken for the Turkey Vulture,
which has a bare red head and no
white patches. The Snail Kite has a
white rump; finer hooked bill, red in
color at the base; and longer red legs.
In flight, the wings are elongated and
without a white patch. Juveniles might
be mistaken for subadults of the Red-
tailed Hawk, which have narrower

Juv.

wings and tail, and lack the light patch under the wings. The juvenile Broad-winged Hawk is smaller, with short wings and is much paler below.

STATUS, DISTRIBUTION, AND HABITATS: Widely distributed along Cuban coasts and adjacent cays. Common in swamps, coastal forests, mangroves, and beaches.

FEEDING: Crabs, amphibians, small snakes, and birds.

NESTING: January-July, mainly April through June. Nest large, built with long branches in moderate-height trees. *Eggs:* 1-4, 2.2" x 1" (56 x 24.6 mm), elliptical, olive cream color, spotted brown or pale purple toward one end.

REFERENCE LOCALITIES:
W PR: Guanahacabibes peninsula; Puerto Esperanza (Viñales); **Mt:** Ciénaga de Zapata (Las Salinas),

Hicacos peninsula, Varadero. **C VC:** Cayo Ensenachos; **CA:** Cayo Coco; **Cm:** Cayo Sabinal and Cayo Romano; **IJ:** Southern part of Isla de la Juventud.

NOTES

Zapata Rail (ZARA)
Cyanolimnas cerverai
Gallinuela de Santo Tomás,
Gallinuela sin Cola,
Gallineta de Zapata (SEO)

IDENTIFICATION: 11.5" (29 cm).
Overall olive-brown pattern, without
spots on the body. Bill long and
green, red at the base. Legs and
iris red. Upperparts olive-brown,
ventral parts gray. Throat white,
light supercilliary line. Flanks with
inconspicuous gray bars. Weak flight.
Juvenile: Paler, without red on the
beak; olivaceous legs. Very little is
known about the Zapata Rail's natural
history and distribution. Few people
have heard or observed it.

VOICE: Unknown. Recordings in
the first edition of the CD *Cantos
de las Aves de Cuba (Bird Calls of
Cuba)* (Reynard and Garrido, 1988)
were recently identified as those of the
Spotted Rail (*Pardirallus maculatus*).

SIMILAR SPECIES: The Spotted Rail is
darker, with spots on the upperparts,
neck, and chest; barred white on
ventral part; and lemon-green bill, with
red at the lower base.

STATUS, DISTRIBUTION, AND HABITATS:
Endemic genus: threatened, rare,
and local. Known only in Ciénaga de
Zapata, around Laguna del Tesoro,
Santo Tomás, Peralta, and Tao de
Jicarita. Its original distribution
apparently extended to other regions of
Cuba. Some fossil remains from Pinar
del Río, Havana, and Isla de la Juventud
are known. Occurs in flooded fresh

water savannas that have an abundance of dense and entangled sawgrass (*Cladium jamaicense*) and isolated trees and shrubs. The introduction of the African sharptooth catfish is a threat to the Rail.

FEEDING: Unknown, probably invertebrate larvae, aquatic snails, and small vertebrates.

NESTING: Unknown, probably November through January. There is a single record that is doubtful. *Eggs:* Unknown.

REFERENCE LOCALITIES:

W **Mt:** Ciénaga de Zapata, Santo Tomás, near Laguna del Tesoro, Hato de Jicarita, and Hatiguanico.

NOTES

Blue-headed Quail-Dove
(BHQD)
Starnoenas cyanocephala
Paloma Perdiz, Paloma Perdiz Cubana
(SEO)

IDENTIFICATION: 12"-13" (30-33 cm). Appearance and posture of a small hen, stockier than other Cuban terrestrial doves. Overall olive-cinnamon brown, darker in the upperparts and with metallic blue crown. Black mask that runs through the eyes. Conspicuous white maxillary band. Broad black and iridescent blue patch on the chest, edged white and with mauve iridescent tones. Sides of neck striated. Beak cadmium red at the base, otherwise grey. Legs coral red. *Juvenile:* Similar, but with dark spots on the crown. Terrestrial habits, although at times perches on trunks, often above 24 feet (8 meters), from where it vocalizes frequently. Usually found in pairs. Congregations of up to 18 individuals have been observed around small pools of water during the dry season. An exquisite ground dove with no marked sexual dimorphism.

VOCALIZATION: *UuuuuuUP,* melancholic, low, and repeated many times.

SIMILAR SPECIES: None.

STATUS, DISTRIBUTION, AND HABITATS: Endemic genus. Originally common, but its populations have drastically decreased since the middle of the 19th century. Now locally common in certain zones such as Guanahacabibes, La Güira, and Zapata peninsula. Rare on Isla de la Juventud. Occurs in dense, shady forests with abundant cover, rocky ground, and ample leaf litter, preferably in flat areas.

FEEDING: Seeds, small fruits, and land snails.

NESTING: April-July. Crude nest built with small branches and leaves, 0-26 feet above ground, on tree stumps, branches, bromeliads, among forks of branches or roots, or vines entangled on the ground. *Eggs:* 2, 1.26"x 1.0" (32.1 x 25.5 mm), white and elliptical.

REFERENCE LOCALITIES:
W **PR:** La Güira, Guanahacabibes: La Jaula, La Pimienta; Sierra de los Órganos; Viñales; **Ar:** Soroa, Loma El Taburete, Nortey, El Mulo; **Mb:** Escaleras de Jaruco; **Mt:** Ciénaga de Zapata; Bermejas, Soplillar. **C** Ciego de Ávila, Loma de Cunagua; **Cm:** Sierra de Cubitas. **E** **Gr:** Cabo Cruz, Sierra Maestra; **SC:** Baconao.

NOTES

Gray-fronted Quail-Dove
(GFQD)
Gray-headed Quail-Dove (GHQD)
Geotrygon caniceps
Camao, Paloma Camá or Casmá,
Azulona, Paloma Perdiz Camao (SEO)

IDENTIFICATION: 11" (28 cm). Overall grayish, upperparts cinnamon brown with highly conspicuous glossy mauve sheen. Rump iridescent blue. Ventral parts gray with cinnamon belly. Head gray with ashy-white forehead. Dark ashy-gray neck with mauve, violet, and green iridescence. Tail blackish; legs and bill red. One of the most beautiful doves in Cuba. An elusive bird, usually found solitary or in pairs, walking through shady patches on the ground where it is difficult to detect.

VOICE: *Uh uh uh uh uuh uuuh.*
A hollow sound, continuous and consistent, that gradually decelerates; vocalization is faster and shorter than that of the Ruddy Quail-Dove. Usually vocalizes when perched.

SIMILAR SPECIES: Most Cuban terrestrial doves are brown and have white lines on the face, and with the exception of the Blue-headed Quail-Dove, the others do not have any blue.

STATUS, DISTRIBUTION, AND HABITATS: Not common. Occurs in dense, humid, shady forests with abundant leaf litter and little human disturbance. At times shares habitat with the Ruddy Quail-Dove, the Key West Quail-Dove, and the Blue-headed Quail-Dove.

FEEDING: Fruits, seeds, and small invertebrates found on the forest floor.

E **Ho:** La Caridad in Pinares de Mayarí, Cerro de Yaguajay, Playa Guardalavaca, Silla de Gibara, Cupeycillo, Baconal, Sierra Cristal.

NOTES

NESTING: January-August. Constructs a crude nest with small branches and leaves at 3 to 12 feet (1-4 meters) from the ground, on trunks, tree branches or palm fronds, especially *guano de costa*. *Eggs:* 1-2 , 1.5"x 2" (33.7 x 25.8 mm), oval and cream colored.

REFERENCE LOCALITIES:
W **PR:** Guanahacabibes, La Güira, Viñales; **Mt:** Punta de Maya, Ciénaga de Zapata: Bermejas, Soplillar, Molina, Bodega Vieja, Santo Tomás.
C **Cm:** Najasa, Sierra de Cubitas.

Bare-legged Owl (BLOW)
Margarobyas lawrencii
Sijú Cotunto, Cotunto, Cuco,
Autillo Cubano (SEO)

IDENTIFICATION: 8"-9" (20-23 cm). Dark brown upperparts with white spots. Breast and belly white with brown vertical markings. Head large. Tail short. Eyes dark brown. Legs unfeathered, relatively long, reddish yellow color. Bill lead-gray. *Female:* Slightly larger than the male. Nocturnal; during the day stays inside cavities in trees or caves. Usually found in pairs. Its flight is short.

VOICE: *Cu cu cu cucucucucu,* low and hollow, repeated more than 12 times, resembling the cadence of a bouncing ball, accelerating toward the end, alternating with slow and short sounds *HUh HUh Huh.*

SIMILAR SPECIES: The Burrowing Owl is not arboreal, is more barred white on the chest, has long, feathered legs, and yellow iris. The Cuban Pygmy Owl is much smaller, with feathered tarsi, legs and iris yellow; dark marks behind the head; diurnal activity.

STATUS, DISTRIBUTION, AND HABITATS: Endemic genus: common throughout mainland Cuba and Isla de la Juventud; rare on Coco, Romano, Guajaba, and Sabinal cays. Occurs in dense and well-preserved forests, coffee plantations, and tree plantations near natural vegetation.

FEEDING: Large insects, frogs, reptiles, small birds, and mammals.

NESTING: December-June, primarily March through May. Does not build

NOTES

a nest; uses holes abandoned by woodpeckers, natural cavities in trees, palms, caves, and rocks. *Eggs:* 2-3 (usually 2), 1.25"x 1.1" (32 x 27 mm), white and nearly round.

REFERENCE LOCALITIES:

W **PR:** Guanahacabibes, Cueva Las Perlas in La Bajada, Viñales, La Güira; **Ar:** Sierra de Anafe; **Mt:** Ciénaga de Zapata: Soplillar, Pálpite, Bermejas. **C** **SS:** Topes de Collantes; **Cm:** Najasa, Sierra de Cubitas. **E** **Ho:** Silla de Gibara, Cupeycillo, Los Hoyos, Sierra Cristal; **Gr:** Baire, Los Negros, La Tabla, Ciénaga de Birama; **SC:** Sierra Maestra, Gran Piedra; **Gt:** Yunque de Baracoa, Nuevo Mundo.

Cuban Pygmy Owl (CUPO)
Glaucidium siju
Sijú Platanero, Sijucito, Cigüita,
Monterita, Cotuntico, Sirigua
Tronconera, Mochuelo Sijú (SEO)

IDENTIFICATION: 6.5"- 7" (17-17.5 cm).
Small and compact body. Upperparts
brown with whitish markings. White
dots on the head. Cinnamon-colored
zone on nape, with black and white
oceli. Tail short, brown with transverse
whitish bands. Underparts barred
cinnamon over white background,
more accentuated toward the flanks
and with a more strongly colored area
toward the chest. Iris yellow. Legs
yellow, short, strong, and covered with
white feathers. Bill yellowish-ochre.
Female: More colorful, a little larger
than the male, with a ferruginous patch
on tarsal feathers, breast, and sides of
head. An inquisitive bird that allows
approach closer than 6 feet (2 meters).
Found in pairs or solitary. Often lifts
its tail moving it sideways and up and
down rapidly. Can turn its head almost
180 degrees. Flight short and direct.
Other species commonly mob the owl
with vigorous jabbering.

VOICE: High-pitched notes gradually
increasing in intensity and speed:
*uh-uh-uh-uh-uh wiu-wiu-wiu-
wiuwiuwiuwiuwiushushushu uh uh
uh-t'chii, t'chwiii swu t'chwiii tswuu.*
Vocalization is common during diurnal
activity.

GEOGRAPHIC VARIATION: (1) *G. s. siju*
(mainland Cuba), and (2) *G. s. vittatum*
(Isla de la Juventud). The individuals
located at Pico Turquino tend to be
stockier and dark.

SIMILAR SPECIES: The Bare-legged Owl
is larger, with big brown eyes, belly
with fine vertical markings, and flesh-
colored bare legs. The Burrowing Owl
is terrestrial.

Juv.

STATUS, DISTRIBUTION, AND HABITATS:
Common. Widely distributed
throughout mainland Cuba, Isla de
la Juventud, and some cays to the
north of Camagüey: Cayo Coco, Cayo
Romano, and Cayo Cantiles. Occurs in
all types of forests (natural, secondary,
and reforested), from sea level to the
mountains.

FEEDING: Terrestrial and arboreal
lizards, large insects (such as moths
and beetles), small and medium-sized
birds.

NESTING: December-May, mainly
March through May. Natural cavities
in trees, or holes abandoned by
woodpeckers. *Eggs:* 3-4, 1.12" x 0.952"
(28.4 x 24.2 mm), plain white, elliptical,
almost round.

REFERENCE LOCALITIES: Forests
throughout Cuba.

NOTES

Cuban Nightjar

Antrostomus cubanensis
(formerly Greater Antillean Nightjar,
GANI, *Rostomus cubanensis*)
Guabairo, Chotacabra Cubana (SEO)

IDENTIFICATION: 11" (28 cm). Grayish-brown with fine black irregular markings, spotted white on chest. Bill short with long decurved bristles. Rounded wings and tail. *Male:* Outer tail feathers marked with white, darker in the female. A difficult bird to observe because it does not call during the day and its cryptic feather pattern closely matches the substrate where it perches, generally on the ground or branches. Usually adopts a longitudinal position in which it remains for long periods. Flies abruptly when an intruder approaches. Commonly perches on posts and fences during the night.

VOICE: *Wurrr wurrr wurrr wurr wurr.* It can be heard at sundown and at night. At daybreak it issues various shorter vocalizations: *qwaoo qwaoo, check check check* or a low sound (*trrrrrrrrrrr*) similar to the purring of a cat.

GEOGRAPHIC VARIATION: Individuals from Isla de la Juventud population are smaller.

SIMILAR SPECIES: The Chuck-will's-widow has a completely different song (*chuc-wills-widow*), is larger, reddish-brown, and without white spots on the chest. The Antillean Nighthawk is less robust and has a rounded head, white throat, and narrower wings, with white-spotted underparts (in flight), and bifurcated tail. Its song is different (*kerqueté-kerequeteé*). The Nighthawk is a summer resident and flies in open spaces in the late afternoon. The Whip-poor-will is very scarce, smaller, and

pale, with more white on face, neck, and tail.

STATUS, DISTRIBUTION, AND HABITATS:
Crepuscular-nocturnal. Common, but difficult to observe. Occurs in moderately dense forests throughout Cuba, Isla de la Juventud, and some cays to the north of Ciego de Ávila and Camagüey.

FEEDING: Insects captured in flight.

NESTING: March-July. *Eggs:* 2, creamy or greenish-gray, variegated with light brown, laid directly on leaf-covered ground. They closely match the substrate.

REFERENCE LOCALITIES:
W **PR:** La Güira, Viñales; **Ar:** Soroa; **Hb:** Jardín Botánico Nacional; **Mt:** Ciénaga de Zapata. **C** **Cm:** Najasa, Sierra de Cubitas. **E** **Ho:** Silla de Gibara, Cupeycillo, Pinares de Mayarí, Sierra Cristal; **Gt:** Nuevo Mundo.

NOTES

Bee Hummingbird (BEEH)
Mellisuga helenae
Pájaro Mosca, Trovador, Colibrí,
Zunzuncito (SEO)

IDENTIFICATION: 2.5" (6.4 cm). The smallest bird in the world. Sexually dimorphic. *Male:* Smaller than the female, ultramarine blue and metallic turquoise upperparts. Belly grayish with darker streaks, and flecks of iridescent dark blue toward the sides. Wings dark. Very short, rounded tail, metallic blue above, tipped with black. Head with ruby-red metallic colored feathers that change appearance according to the direction of the light, at times appearing very dark with a metallic sheen. Throat the same color, with very conspicuous elongated feathers during breeding period. *Female:* Upperparts metallic turquoise blue combined with green tones, paler than in the male. Belly gray and tail blue with white patch at the end; whitish supercilliary line. *Juvenile:* Similar to the female, young males are blue with greenish tones above, head with a crown of dark feathers and throat with gray stripes and black spine. As it matures and reaches breeding season, darker feathers appear on the head and throat, ruby colored feathers spread out farther reaching the shoulders. Tail feathers black at the extreme tip. Aggressive and territorial. During courtship the male performs characteristic U-shaped aerial displays, interspersed with perching on the tallest twigs. Forages on flowers in an almost horizontal position.

VOICE: High-pitched, sharp, very noisy, and with a metallic tone, extremely strong for such a small bird: *stwi stwi swi swi swi shweit, sriiiiiiiii… swe swe swe shew shew sriiiiiiiii… srwee swreee swe.*

SIMILAR SPECIES: The Ruby-throated Hummingbird is larger, upperparts

♂   ♂   ♂ Juv.   ♂

greener, the tail is clearly forked. The Cuban Emerald is much larger, with iridescent emerald green upperparts, tail long.

STATUS, DISTRIBUTION, AND HABITATS: Rare, occurs from coastal scrub vegetation to mountain forests, at times in gardens and other open areas. Frequently in forest edges with abundance of shrubs and flowers. Fragmented populations in Cuba and Isla de la Juventud. More common in Ciénaga de Zapata and in the east (Guantánamo and Holguín). Accidental in New Providence Island in the Bahamas.

FEEDING: Nectar, but also small insects and arachnids.

NESTING: March-June. Nest cup-like, similar to the Cuban Emerald. Built of cotton, grass, hair, and other soft materials, covered with lichens and spiderwebs, at about 8 feet (2.5 meters) from the ground. *Eggs:* 2, 0.5" x 0.4" (11.1 x 8 mm), white.

REFERENCE LOCALITIES:
W PR: Guanahacabibes: Cabo de San Antonio, Cabo Corrientes; **Ar:** Sierra de Anafe; **Mt:** Ciénaga de Zapata: Santo Tomás, Pálpite, Soplillar, Bermejas. **C SS:** Topes de Collantes, Jobo Rosado; **Cm:** Najasa. **E Ho:** Gibara, Sierra Cristal, Cayo Guan, Farallones de Moa, Nuevo Mundo, Jaguaní; **SC:** Siboney; **Gt:** Parque Humboldt, Ojito de Agua, Cruzata, Cayo Probado, El Bagá, Baitiquirí.

NOTES

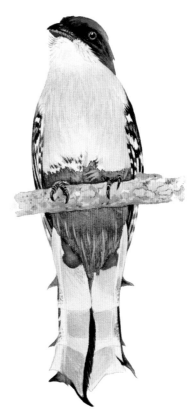

Cuban Trogon (CUTR)
Priotelus temnurus
Tocororo, Tocoloro, Toroloco, Guatiní,
Trogón Tocororo (SEO)

IDENTIFICATION: 10"-11" (25-28 cm). No sexual dimorphism. Belly grayish-white, whiter toward the throat. Conspicuous and brilliant red ventral patch makes it unmistakable. Iridescent upperparts. Emerald green, sometimes appearing iridescent deep blue above. Head blue with a violet sheen and black mask running through the eyes from the bill, not clearly visible in the field. Wings blackish-brown, speckled with iridescent blue and alternate white spots. Bill strong and serrated, red and dark brown. Iris red. The undertail has white patches alternating with blue iridescent tones. Tail with greenish-bronze and purplish tones above, edges truncated. Flight short and undulating. Stays motionless for long periods. Perches solitary or in pairs at moderate height from the ground, usually higher than 6 feet (2 meters), with a characteristic posture and frequent vocalization. One of the most beautiful Cuban birds. Because its color pattern is reminiscent of the Cuban flag, it is designated the national bird of Cuba.

VOICE: Rapid and guttural: *To-roro to-roro to-roro, toc toc-toc tororororoooo toc-torororoor tot tot gcuaw gcuwau gcwau*. Occasionally emits guttural sounds, making it difficult to locate.

GEOGRAPHIC VARIATION: Individuals from Isla de la Juventud are smaller and their belly patch is slightly paler.

SIMILAR SPECIES: None.

STATUS, DISTRIBUTION, AND HABITATS: Widely distributed throughout Cuba, Isla de la Juventud, and the larger cays to the north of

Camagüey (Guajaba, Romano, and Sabinal). Common from coastal zones to the mountains, in all forest types, mainly in the more humid and shady areas.

FEEDING: Fruits, flowers, insects, and reptiles. Consumption of the last two increases during the reproductive period.

NESTING: February-August, mainly April through July. Uses abandoned nests of woodpeckers and natural holes in trees. *Eggs:* 3-4, 1"x 0.85" (27.6 x 21.4 mm), elliptical to oval, white.

REFERENCE LOCALITIES:
W PR: Guanahacabibes, Viñales, La Güira; **Ar:** Las Terrazas, Soroa; **Mt:** Ciénaga de Zapata. **C Cf:** Topes de Collantes, Finca Cudina; **Cm:** Najasa, Sierra de Cubitas.

E Ho: Silla de Gibara, Cupeycillo, Pinares de Mayarí, Cabonico, Sagua de Tánamo, Sierra Cristal; **Gr:** Santo Domingo; **SC:** Gran Piedra; **Gt:** El Yunque de Baracoa, Parque Humboldt.

NOTES

Cuban Tody (CUTO)
Todus multicolor
Cartacuba, Pedorrera, Barrancorrío,
Barrancolí Cubano (SEO)

IDENTIFICATION: 4.45" (10.8 cm).
Small, chubby, without visible sexual
dimorphism. Head large. Neck and
tail short. Bill long, flat, red below and
dark brown above. Upperparts brilliant
green. Belly pale gray with crimson red
patch on throat. Cheeks with pale blue
patch. Sides of belly pink. Undertail
coverts pale lemon yellow. Iris light
blue in the adult and brown in juvenile.
Usually waits for its prey from a perch.
The Tody's coloration and small size
make it difficult to see perched in
vegetation, but it vocalizes frequently,
which facilitates detection. It is
inquisitive, coming near or allowing
people to approach closely. During
the breeding season its belly becomes
stained with the color of the earth in
which it excavates its nest. Flight low
and rapid. It is one of the most frequent
and charismatic endemic bird species
in Cuban forests.

VOICE: Strong, rapid, and sustained call:
*tot-tot-tot-tot tottottottot tot-tot-tot-
tot tottottottottot tot tot prrrrrrrrree*,
repeated many times and alternating in
speed. In flight it makes a characteristic
sound with its wings.

STATUS, DISTRIBUTION, AND HABITATS:
Widely distributed in Cuba, Isla de
la Juventud, and the larger cays to
the north of Camagüey and Ciego de
Ávila. Commonly occurs in wooded
or semi-wooded vegetation, from
the mountains to sea level. It may be
observed at times in the mangroves
adjacent to coastal forests.

FEEDING: Insectivorous, highly
voracious, can eat almost 40% of its
own weight per day. Its diet consists
of larvae, small insects, caterpillars,
spiders, small fruits, and small reptiles,

for which it searches while perched on a branch, then flies a short distance to catch them, returning to the same perch.

NESTING: April-July. Excavates tunnel-like holes, about 10" deep by 1" in diameter (25 x 2.5 cm), with a chamber at the far end. Builds its nest in banks on the sides of roads; in mounds of earth or sand; in live or dead tree trunks; and in natural cavities of limestone and other substrates. At times it uses the holes made by land crabs. Generally excavates more than one opening near the main entrance. *Eggs:* 3-5, 0.6"x 0.45" (15.5 x 11.6 mm), white, elliptical to oval.

REFERENCE LOCALITIES:
W **PR:** Guanahacabibes, Viñales, La Güira; **Ar:** Soroa; **Hb:** Jardín Botánico Nacional; **Mt:** Ciénaga de Zapata.
C **SS:** Topes de Collantes, Finca Cudina; **Cm:** Najasa, Sierra de Cubitas.

E **Ho:** Pinares de Mayarí, Cerro de Yaguajay, Guardalavaca, Silla de Gibara, Cupeycillo, El Yayal, Mirador de Mayabe, Moa; **Gr:** Santo Domingo; **SC:** Gran Piedra, La Mula, Siboney; **Gt:** Parque Humboldt, Santa María, El Yunque de Baracoa.

NOTES

♂

Cuban Green Woodpecker
(CGWO)
Xiphidiopicus percussus
Carpintero Verde, Guasusa, Tajá,
Jorré Jorré, Ruán
Carpintero Tajá (SEO)

IDENTIFICATION: 8"-10" (21-25 cm). The only Cuban woodpecker with green (olive-green) upperparts. Breast and belly variable tones of yellow with blackish lines on the chest and barred flanks. Sides of face white with a black band behind the eyes. Crest elevated at will. *Male:* Crown and throat red. *Female:* Posterior crown red with the anterior half black, marked with white flecks, throat red. *Juvenile:* Duller, with black throat patch, and black on crown and chest. Coloration and size vary depending on populations.

VOICE: *Tajá tajá tajá-cwac-cwac.*

GEOGRAPHIC VARIATION: *X. p. percussus* (Cuba and Conuco, Tío Pepe, and Lanzanillo cays), *X. p. insulaepinorum* (Isla de la Juventud and some adjacent cays). Other subspecies have been described; apparently there is a gradual change in certain characteristics exhibited by a tendency to size increase and coloration intensification toward the mountains; coastal populations have duller colors.

SIMILAR SPECIES: The Yellow-bellied Sapsucker is smaller, plumage white and black without green upperparts.

STATUS, DISTRIBUTION, AND HABITATS: Endemic genus. Cuba, Isla de la Juventud, and some cays north and

♀

Juv.

south of the island. The most common woodpecker in the archipelago's forests. Occurs from sea level (mangroves) to the mountains. Accidental in Jamaica and Hispaniola.

FEEDING: Insects, spiders, and scorpions, captured by climbing around trunks and branches; also small fruits and frogs. Occasionally feeds on nectar from certain large plants.

NESTING: January-August, primarily March through May. Cavities bored in live or dead trunks, narrow entrance at 3-36 feet (2-12 m) above the ground.

Eggs: 3-4, 1" x 0.75" (25.9 x 18.3 mm), white, oval, and smooth.

REFERENCE LOCALITIES: Common in all natural forests.

NOTES

♀

Fernandina's Flicker (FEFL)
Colaptes fernandinae
Carpintero Churroso, Carpintero
de Tierra, Carpintero Hormiguero,
Carpintero Hediondo,
Carpintero Churroso (SEO)

IDENTIFICATION: 13"-14" (33-35 cm).
With the exception of the Ivory-
billed Woodpecker, this is the
largest woodpecker in Cuba. Overall
yellowish-brown, finely barred black,
with cinnamon hue on the head.
Underwing and tail yellow. Legs
lead-gray to blackish. *Male:* Black
"mustache" behind the commissures,
absent in the female. The only
woodpecker in Cuba lacking red color.
Often forages on the ground. Most
frequently found in pairs during the
breeding season, when it may group in
colonies of up to 15 pairs. The rest of
the year it is usually solitary.

VOICE: *Píic píic píic-píuc píuc píuc-
picpicpicpic trrrrrrrrrrrrr,* dry and
sharp.
SIMILAR SPECIES: The West Indian
Woodpecker has red on the head,
more white on the body and two white
underwing patches. The Northern
Flicker has a black patch on the chest
and spots on the belly, head gray and
red patch on the nape in both sexes.
STATUS, DISTRIBUTION, AND HABITATS:
The rarest woodpecker in Cuba after
the Ivory-billed Woodpecker. Locally
common in some areas, patchily
distributed. Occurs primarily in
savannas with palms, marshy sites, and
open forests. Accidental in Bahamas.
FEEDING: Ants and insect larvae, usually

♂

♀

♀

NOTES

obtained from the ground where it probes and excavates with its bill. Occasionally small fruits and seeds.

NESTING: February-June. Excavates its nest in palms and dead or dying trees with soft wood, in a descending shallow hole. The nest may be located close to the ground. Nest is used successively for several years. *Eggs:* 4-5, 1"x 0.8" (26 x 20 mm), white.

REFERENCE LOCALITIES:

W PR: Sierra del Rosario, Tibisí, Minas de Matahambre; **Ar:** Soroa; **Mt:** Bermejas in Zapata peninsula. **C Cf:** Hills around Trinidad; Santa Clara suburbs; **VC:** El Dorado, Corralillo; **Cm:** Najasa. **E Gr:** Ciénaga de Birama; **SC:** La Tabla.

Psittacidae

Cuban Macaw (CUBM)
Ara tricolor
Guacamayo Cubano

IDENTIFICATION: 20" (50 cm). Extinct. Medium-sized, tri-colored macaw, smaller and more slender than Scarlet Macaw (*Ara macao*) from Central and South America. Cadmium-reddish-orange overall, with yellow on crown and hindneck. Massive black bill. Rump, and upper and under-tail coverts blue. Wing coverts with a blood-brown patch, edged with green in juveniles.

VOICE: Unknown.

STATUS, DISTRIBUTION, AND HABITATS: Became extinct in the second half of the 19th century; the last known individual was killed in 1864 in the forest surrounding the Ciénaga de Zapata. Originally it was distributed throughout Cuba and Isla de la Juventud. At least two similar species supposedly inhabited Jamaica and Dominican Republic, but no specimens of those species are known to exist; nevertheless, there are historical

Juv.

accounts from Hispaniola. Its extinction was caused by the felling of nesting trees to capture young birds for pets, and hunting for food.

NESTING: Unknown.

COMMENTS: Although extinct, the macaw is represented here based on a reconstruction of the bird from 16 specimens located in international collections.

Cuban Parakeet (CPAK)
Psittacara euops
Catey, Periquito, Perico,
Aratinga Cubana (SEO)

IDENTIFICATION: 9.5"-10.5" (25-27 cm). Brilliant green with small isolated red spots on the head, sides of neck, and chest. In flight, the red patches in the coverts and the golden color of the underwings are evident. Tail long and pointed. Iris with yellow ring. Bill flesh colored. *Juvenile:* Paler than the adult and with few or no red spots, which begin to appear after the first year. Gregarious and nomadic. Forms medium to large flocks of approximately 12 to 30 individuals; notorious for their chattering while moving from one place to another. Commonly observed in pairs during the breeding season. Green color makes it difficult to detect while perched in foliage. Timid and does not allow close approach.

VOICE: *Crew crew crew,* repeated many times while flying. When perched or feeding it makes a similar murmur but in lower tones.

SIMILAR SPECIES: None.

STATUS, DISTRIBUTION, AND HABITATS: Occurs only on mainland Cuba. Extirpated on the Isla de la Juventud. Populations have drastically decreased range-wide because of destruction of habitats and capture as pets. However, still common in some localities like Ciénaga de Zapata, mountains of Trinidad, Najasa, Ciénaga de Birama, and La Melba. Occurs in secondary forests, and in savannas with palms, within or close to marshes.

FEEDING: Seeds, fruits, sprouts, and flowers.

NESTING: March-September, primarily April through May. Does not build a nest; uses holes abandoned by woodpeckers in trunks of dead palms and other tree cavities. More than one pair may nest in one trunk. Occasionally uses cliff or cave cavities. *Eggs:* 2-5, 1.5"x 0.75" (33 x 18.5 mm), white and elliptical.

REFERENCE LOCALITIES:

W **Mt:** Ciénaga de Zapata. **C** **Cf:** Valle de Yaguanabo, Topes de Collantes; **CA:** Júcaro; **SS:** Banao, Ciénaga de Guayaberas; **Cm:** Loma de Cunagua, Vertientes, Najasa. **E** **LT:** Monte Cabaniguán cerca de Sabalo; **Gr:** Sabanalamar in Ciénaga de Birama; **Ho:** La Melba, Pico Cristal.

NOTES

Cuban Vireo (CUVI)
Vireo gundlachii
Juan Chiví Ojón, Chichinguao,
Ojón, Pichijú, Vireo Cubano
(SEO)

IDENTIFICATION: 5.25" (13 cm).
Body more compact than a
warbler and with a stronger bill that
is elongated and flesh-colored, with
brown above. Eyes dark brown and
large. Overall, grayish-olive green
upperparts, pale yellowish underparts.
Light ring around the eyes. Wings with
pale bars. *Juvenile:* Paler and duller.
Common in forests where it occurs
mainly in pairs or solitary. At times
found in mixed flocks with the Yellow-
headed Warbler or the Oriente Warbler.
Flies short distances within vegetation
where it perches and forages at about
3 to 10 feet (1-3 meters) above the
ground. Because of its dull coloration,
it is difficult to detect, although its song
makes it easier to locate.

VOICE: *Wí-shiví shíw wí shiví shíw wi
shí shiw wi shí show t´wiií wiu
chechechecheche twit wuiu*, a rapid,
high-pitched, and varied whistle. It may
be mistaken for the Black-whiskered
Vireo, a common summer resident that
has similar vocalization.

GEOGRAPHIC VARIATION: *V. g. gundlachii*
(from Pinar del Río to Camagüey and
Isla de la Juventud); *V. g. orientalis* (east,
from Camagüey); *V. g. magnus* (Cayo
Cantiles); *V. g. sanfelipensis* (Cayo Real,
Cayo San Felipe, Cayo Pinar del Río).

SIMILAR SPECIES: The Yellow-throated
Vireo and the Blue-headed Vireo have
white and yellow lines from the beak
to behind the eyes, and distinct white
bars on wings. The Black-whiskered
Vireo has lighter underparts and white

eyebrow stripes, dark eyelines, and black mustache stripes.

STATUS, DISTRIBUTION, AND HABITATS: Common. Cuba, Isla de la Juventud, and some large cays to the north and south of the island. Occurs in all types of natural and secondary forests, coffee plantations, pine groves, and shrubby vegetation, from sea level to the mountains.

FEEDING: Insects, spiders, fruits, and small reptiles.

NESTING: March-August, mainly April through June. Nest is a hanging cup in forks of branches, made with grass, hairs, moss, lichens, roots, and small feathers, lined with softer materials. *Eggs:* 3, 0.78"x 0.54" (19.8 x 13.8 mm), white, mottled with chestnut colored dots, oval to elongated oval.

REFERENCE LOCALITIES: Common in all Cuban forests.

NOTES

Zapata Wren (ZAWR)
Ferminia cerverai
Fermina, Ratona de Zapata (SEO)

IDENTIFICATION: 6.25" (16 cm). Sexes similar. Tail, bill, and legs long. Wings short and rounded. Overall color cinnamon-brown, upperparts and tail finely streaked with black, darker toward the head. Belly brownish-white, striated toward the rear of the belly and undertail coverts. While vocalizing the yellow throat color may be visible; tail is held low. A very secretive bird, difficult to locate. Flight short. Usually vanishes into the grasses when intruders are present. Best detected early in the morning, between 7:00 and 8:30 a.m., especially on days without wind.

VOICE: Difficult to describe onomatopoetically. High, very musical and sharp, somewhat similar to a canary's song; lower and shorter in females, with metallic tones in the middle or end. Considered one of the best songbirds in the West Indies.

SIMILAR SPECIES: The House Wren is smaller, lighter, and less streaked on upperparts and underparts. Tail shorter, light supercilliary line. Does not occur in sawgrass.

STATUS, DISTRIBUTION, AND HABITAT: Endemic genus. Rare and occurs only in marsh grasses: cattail, sawgrass, and shrubs of the western part of Zapata. Its distribution there is not well known. Fires that destroy large patches of sawgrass (*Cladium jamaicense*) and cattail flag (*Typha angustifolia*) have adversely affected this species. Rats, mongooses, and African sharptooth catfish are also a threat.

FEEDING: Insects, caterpillars, spiders, small fruits, and small lizards.

NESTING: January-July, mainly March through May. Nest constructed of dry

grasses and lined with vegetable fiber and feathers, placed from 1 to 3.3 feet (0.30-1 meter) above the ground and well-concealed among grasses. Its structure and coloring make it indistinguishable from the vegetation. Nest globular, with a 1.6" (41 mm) side entrance similar to that of grassquits and bullfinches. *Eggs:* 2, white.

REFERENCE LOCALITIES:
W Mt: Western Zapata peninsula: Peralta, Santo Tomás, Río Negro, Hato de Jicarita, Guareira, Zanja La Cocodrila, Canal de los Patos, La Yuca, Hatiguanico river basin.

NOTES

Cuban Gnatcatcher (CUGN)
Polioptila lembeyei
Sinsontillo, Perlita Cubana (SEO)

IDENTIFICACIÓN: 4.5" (11 cm). Small, graceful, and vivacious. Bill long and slender. Bluish-gray upperparts and grayish-white underparts. Tail long, usually cocked upwards, with white outer feathers. Narrow black crescent design from the eyes to behind the auriculars, thicker in the male. White eye ring. *Juvenile:* Pale with an olivaceous hue, auricular marking faint.

VOCALIZATION: Low, begins with: *Ship ship ship fuiii-shipshipship fui ship*, incorporating very diverse notes. Complex and elaborate melodious repertoire, difficult to describe; somewhat similar to the Zapata Wren.

SIMILAR SPECIES: Can be mistaken for the Blue-gray Gnatcatcher, which is slightly larger and robust, paler, and with a black supercilliary. Does not have the black marking behind the eye and ear coverts. The song is very different and not so melodious. Occurs in wooded areas. Winter resident.

STATUS, DISTRIBUTION, AND HABITATS: Locally common, more abundant on the southern coast of Guantánamo. Distributed in isolated locations in central and eastern Cuba from Ciego de Ávila to Maisí, and in Romano, Coco, Guajaba, and Sabinal cays. Occurs in dense and spiny vegetation, in arid coastal zones and interior areas with similar characteristics.

FEEDING: Insects, spiders, and other arthropods.

NESTING: March-July. Nest cup-like, similar but somewhat larger than Bee Hummingbird's, built at low height on horizontal twigs and branches among spiny plants, using horse hairs,

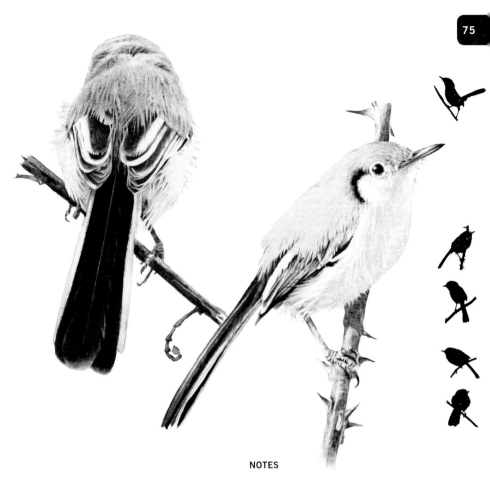

NOTES

vegetable fibers, and small leaves, and lined on the interior and exterior with lichens, spiderwebs, and other soft materials. *Eggs:* 3-5, 0.55" x 0.43" (14 x 11 mm), white, with some dark brown spots.

REFERENCE LOCALITIES:

C Cm: Nuevitas, Santa Lucía, and Najasa; Coco, Romano, Guajaba, and Sabinal cays; **SS:** Southern coast, Casilda, and Trinidad. **E Ho:** Gibara, Asiento Molido, Cerro Galano; costa sur Cabo Cruz; **SC:** Siboney; **Gt:** Maisí, Baitiquirí (Bate Bate), Tortuguilla, Imías.

IUCN **NT** | CUBA **VU**

Cuban Solitaire (CUSO)
Myadestes elisabeth
Ruiseñor, Clarín Cubano (SEO)

IDENTIFICATION: 7.5" (19 cm). Uniform olive-brown upperparts. Sexes similar. Belly gray, similar to the rest of the body. White eye-ring. Dark mandibular line. Bill short and fine. Legs yellow. *Juvenile:* Olive-grayish upperparts, with brown streaked underparts. A difficult bird to locate in the field, even if calling. Remains still for long periods, perched within the foliage at a considerable height. Territorial; usually found in pairs. **VOICE:** Melancholic, melodious, and sharp. May be heard at great distances. Song is difficult to describe: similar to the sound of rubbing wet fingers over the rim of a crystal goblet. The notes start with an almost inaudible trill that gradually increases until the sound becomes very intense and stable. One of the most exquisite songbirds in Cuba.

SIMILAR SPECIES: La Sagra's Flycatcher has feathers on the head that it lifts crest-like. No white around the eyes or on the outer tail feathers. Does not have a dark mandible stripe. It perches mainly on more exposed branches.

STATUS, DISTRIBUTION, AND HABITATS: Near threatened. Montane and premontane zones of western and eastern Cuba, where it is locally common. More abundant in the eastern region. Absent from the center of the island. Occurs in dense and humid forests (semi-deciduous, evergreen, rainforest, gallery forest, and pine groves) in the mountains. Extirpated from Isla de la Juventud

around 1930. Its populations have declined considerably because of deforestation.

FEEDING: Insects, fruits, and seeds snatched in flight similar to the feeding habits of pewees and kingbirds.

NESTING: February-July, mainly February through April. Nest irregular cup-like structure inside a rock or tree cavity. Built with animal and organic fibers, covered with moss, lichens, and other plants. At times, concealed within bromeliads. *Eggs:* 3, pale green, heavily spotted with brown.

REFERENCE LOCALITIES:

W **PR:** Sierra del Rosario, Sierra de la Güira, Sierra de los Órganos, Viñales, Minas de Matahambre. **E** **Ho:** Pinares de Mayarí, Cabonico, Sierra Cristal, Moa, Cupeyal del Norte, Farallones de Moa, Ojito de Agua; **Gr:** Santo Domingo, Pico la Bayamesa; **SC:** Gran Piedra, Pico Turquino; **Gt:** Parque Humboldt, Nuevo Mundo.

NOTES

Yellow-headed Warbler
(YHWA)
Teretistris fernandinae
Chillina, Chinchilita, Chillona,
Chipe de Cabeza Amarilla (SEO)

IDENTIFICATION: 5" (13 cm). Overall color lead-gray with grayish-white belly. Head and neck lemon yellow. Bill long, fine, and slightly decurved. No bars or stripes on its body. *Juvenile:* Upperparts with olivaceous hue. Behavior similar to that of the Oriente Warbler. At times it is the nuclear species of mixed flocks.

VOICE: *She she she she she -shi shi shi shi -chip chip,* repeated many times, reminiscent of that of the Oriente Warbler, especially when several individuals in the group vocalize.

SIMILAR SPECIES: The yellow color of Oriente Warbler extends toward the breast. The Prothonotary Warbler is golden yellow overall with blue-gray wings and tail.

STATUS, DISTRIBUTION, AND HABITATS: Endemic genus. Common in western and central Cuba, from Guanahacabibes north to Itabo in Matanzas, and south to Ciénaga de Zapata; Isla de la Juventud and Cayo Cantiles in the Canarreos archipelago, from sea level to medium elevations. Occurs mainly in shrubby vegetation, open forests with vines, and mangroves.

FEEDING: Insects, spiders and other arthropods, small reptiles, and small fruits. Forages in small flocks from the ground to the canopy.

NESTING: March-July. Nest cup-like, on horizontal twigs and, at times, among parasitic plants inside tangled

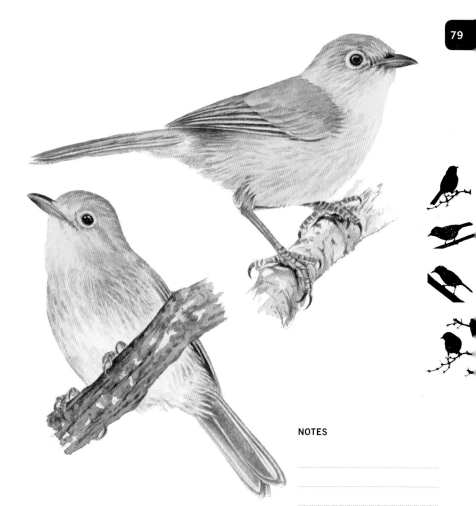

NOTES

vegetation. Made with dry grass, Spanish moss and other bromeliads, small roots, and other plant material; not lined with soft material. *Eggs:* 2-3, 0.77" x 0.51" (19.6 x 13.1 mm), oval/ elongated, white with a light bluish-green tone, and brown or purplish marks toward the broad end.

REFERENCE LOCALITIES:
E **PR:** Viñales, La Güira, Guanahacabibes; **Ar:** Soroa; **Mt:** Ciénaga de Zapata, Varadero, Hicacos peninsula.

Oriente Warbler (ORWA)
Teretistris fornsi
Bijirita Pechero, Pechero, Pecherito,
Che-ché, Chipe de Oriente (SEO)

IDENTIFICATION: 5.25" (13 cm). Body with dull, soft colors; lemon-yellow underparts, steel-gray upperparts. Without dark designs or white marks. Bill fine, slightly decurved and elongated. Sexes similar. A noisy and inquisitive bird when an intruder is detected. Gregarious behavior. Forms medium and small groups. Seen in pairs at breeding time. Flocks may be nuclear to diverse species of warblers, flycatchers, kingbirds, and other migratory species.

VOICE: A metallic *shee shee shee shee sheecheechee -zhit zhit zhitzhit zhitzhit-zhit zhit zhít zhit* gradually increasing in intensity and combined with the vocalizations of other members of the flock.

SIMILAR SPECIES: Similar to the Yellow-headed Warbler, which is slightly smaller and only the head is yellow. The female of the Prothonotary Warbler is more robust. The yellow is overlapped with the gray upperparts. The juvenile of the Yellow Warbler is less conspicuous with pale patches on the wings and a supercilliary line. The Hooded Warbler and Wilson's Warbler have olive-green upperparts and wings. The Canada Warbler is very rare in Cuba and has black marks on the chest. The Blue-winged Warbler has a yellow forehead and slate-gray wings with white patches. These species may occasionally be nuclear in flocks of Oriente Warblers during the fall migration period.

STATUS, DISTRIBUTION, AND HABITATS: Endemic genus. Common, restricted to zones in the central and eastern

provinces. Its distribution area extends along the northern coast of Holguín to Camagüey, Ciego de Ávila and the large adjacent cays, to Itabo in Matanzas Province. Occurs in forests and thickets, from sea level to the mountains.

FEEDING: Forages in small flocks in the canopy, vines, branches, trunk crevices and, occasionally, on the ground. Feeds on larvae, insects, spiders, other arthropods, and small reptiles.

NESTING: April-July. Nest cup-like, of dry leaves, small roots, and other plant fibers, built on twigs within vegetation. *Eggs:* 2-3, 0.75" x 0.55" (19 x 14 mm), white with a very pale greenish hue with purplish and reddish-brown spots toward the broad end.

REFERENCE LOCALITIES:
W Cm: Sierra de Cubitas. **E Ho:** Guardalavaca, Playa Esmeralda, Cerro de Yaguajay, Silla de Gibara, Cupeycillo, Loma La Yaya, Gibara: Caletones; El Yayal, Pinares de Mayarí, Cabonico, Ojito de Agua, Farallones de Moa; **Gr:** Santo Domingo; **SC:** La Mula, Gran Piedra, Sierra Maestra, Pico Turquino.

NOTES

♂

♀

Cuban Grassquit (CUGR)
Tiaris canorus
Tomeguín, Senserenico, Tomeguín del Pinar (SEO)

IDENTIFICATION: 4.5" (11.5 cm). Small bird with a short, thick bill. *Male:* Bright yellow crescent on side of head and throat, bordered with black areas; very flashy. Crown gray. Olivaceous upperparts. Belly and sides dull gray. *Female:* Yellow crescent on head and throat less noticeable, without black border. Sides of the face with a cinnamon mask. *Juvenile:* Similar to the female, coloration duller. Male sub-adults have a black area on the face with chestnut colored spots and a smallish black patch on the breast. Commonly observed in small flocks of 5 to 30 individuals or in pairs during the breeding season. An energetic bird, quickly detected by its song. Frequents gardens and backyards in rural zones.
VOICE: *Wichiri- wichíiira ship -ship -ship –ship-ship tsip tsip pitchiá tsip tsip pichirá pichirá.*

SIMILAR SPECIES: The Yellow-faced Grassquit is more common, has a reduced yellow patch with light orange hue on throat and an extended yellow eyebrow stripe; small yellow-orange infraocular stripe non-existent in the Cuban Grassquit. The upper part of the head is olivaceous, never gray. Shares similar habitats. Song different and less musical (*bpist bpist ptseeeptseeptsee*). The Black-faced Grassquit is rare in Cuba; overall coloration is darker with cinnamon undertail coverts, no yellow patches.
STATUS, DISTRIBUTION, AND HABITATS: Throughout Cuba, but absent from Isla de la Juventud and adjacent cays.

♀

♂ Juv.

♀

Occurs primarily in semiarid zones near coasts, natural or semi-natural forest borders, pine groves and casuarina plantations, shrubby vegetation of spiny and sub-spiny xenomorphic thickets over serpentinite rock, and coastal underbrush. Frequents rural areas and savannas with shrubs, from the coast to medium elevations. Its populations have decreased considerably because of illegal capture and trafficking as a caged bird for its melodious song. Introduced in Florida and New Providence, Bahamas where it is common.

FEEDING: Seeds, small fruits, and sprouts.

NESTING: March-October, mainly April through May. Nest spherical with side entrance, placed lower than 6 feet (2 meters), usually in shrubby and spiny vegetation, and constructed of dry grass, hair, roots, and other soft materials. *Eggs:* 2-3, 0.62" x 0.43" (15.7 x 11 mm), oval, white with a light olive-gray tone, chestnut and purplish dots concentrated around the broad end.

REFERENCE LOCALITIES:
W PR: San Ubaldo, Minas de Matahambre, Viñales, Sierra del Rosario; **Hb:** Jardín Botánico Nacional. **C Cm:** Najasa. **E Ho:** Cupeycillo, Cerro de Yaguajay, Playa de Caletones, Las Azules, Silla de Gibara, Pinares de Mayarí, Cabonico; **Gr:** Santo Domingo.

NOTES

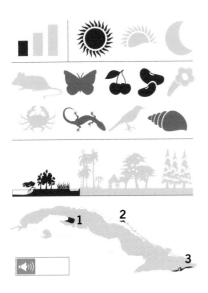

1

Cuban Sparrow
or Zapata Sparrow (ZASP)
Torreornis inexpextata
Cabrerito de la Ciénaga, Cabrerito
Cubano, Sabanero de Zapata (SEO)

IDENTIFICATION: 6.5" (16.5 cm).
Grayish appearance. Belly light yellow.
Sides olive-gray. Crown brown.
Sides of face lead-gray, iris reddish
brown. Throat white, bordered by a
black stripe. Upperparts olive-gray.
Wings disproportionally short and
rounded. Tail long. Bill thick, dark
gray. Legs rose-colored. The eastern
subspecies is duller on crown and belly.
Juvenile: Paler.

VOCALIZATION: *Zrii riii rii rii ri riririr
pit pit pit zrii zrii zrii zrii zriizriizrii
-zrii zrii- zriiireeeee -pit pit pit pit pit
zriii zriii zriii*. High-pitched and noisy
call that increases in intensity.

GEOGRAPHIC VARIATION: (1) *Torreornis
i. inexpectata* (Ciénaga de Zapata);

(2) *T. i. varonai* (Cayo Coco);
(3) *T. i. sigmani* (Southern coast of
Guantánamo).

SIMILAR SPECIES: The female Dickcissel
has striped upperparts, yellowish
eyebrow stripe, and a chestnut colored
patch on shoulders. Breast pale yellow
and bill rose-colored. Chipping Sparrow
lacks the black mustache stripe; breast
is gray, upperparts striated, with white
bands on wings, brown or reddish-
brown on crown.

STATUS, DISTRIBUTION, AND HABITATS:
Endemic genus. The subspecies occupy
different habitats and regions: (1)
temporarily flooded grassland with
shrubs in the western part of Ciénaga de
Zapata; (2) Cayo Coco in dry and semi-
dry forests, shrubs, and coastal thickets
where it is most abundant; (3) Baitiquirí,
the most arid zone in Cuba, amidst semi-

desert vegetation, spiny shrubs, cacti, and isolated trees. From Tortuguilla to west of Laguna de Baconao, which lies in Santiago de Cuba province.

FEEDING: Mainly seeds and small fruits. During the dry season, its diet consists of seeds, flowers, fruits, and vegetable material, occasionally small invertebrates. In the rainy season, includes snail eggs (Pomacea), small mollusks, reptiles, beetles, and cactus fruits. More active from 6:30 to 10:00 a.m.; at midday it shelters in vegetation.

NESTING: March through August. Nest cup-like, woven and concealed among tall grasses, less than three feet above the ground. *Eggs:* 1-2, white with a greenish hue, and reddish, rosy, or brown dots more concentrated toward the broad end.

REFERENCE LOCALITIES:

W Mt: Ciénaga de Zapata: Canal de los Patos, Laguna El Palmar, Cayos de Gervedero, Cayo Corral, Maneadero, Lagunas del Vínculo, Hatiguanico river basin, and Santo Tomás. **C CA:** Cayo Coco. **E Gt:** Baitiquirí (Bate Bate), Imías, Tortuguilla, Cajobabo.

NOTES

Cuban Oriole (CUOR)
Icterus melanopsis
(formerly Greater Antillean Oriole)
Solibio, Guainuba,
Turpial Cubano (SEO)

IDENTIFICATION: 8"-8.5" (20-22 cm). Sexes similar. Overall black with bright yellow patches on the shoulders, rump, and undertail coverts. *Juvenile:* Olive-green, rather than yellow on belly; throat and wings black. Shoulder, rump, and undertail covert patches like adults, but with a greenish-yellow tone. Undulating flight. Frequently found in pairs, perching on the ends of flower spikes. Formerly treated as a subspecies of *I. dominicensis.* At present it is considered a valid species based on genetic, morphological, and vocalization differences.

VOICE: *Check check.* It also has a melodious song, more frequent during the first hours in the morning, made up of a series of varied and complex high-pitched notes.

SIMILAR SPECIES: The Orchard Oriole has black markings in the upperparts; and has white bands on the wings.

STATUS, DISTRIBUTION, AND HABITATS: Common in Cuba, Isla de la Juventud, and some northern cays: Guillermo, Coco, and Paredón Grande. Occurs in natural and secondary forests, gardens, agricultural lands, and other rural areas, from sea level to the mountains.

FEEDING: Fruits, flowers, nectar, and insects.

NESTING: February-July, mainly March through June, irregularly all year round. Nest spherical, highly elaborate and with lateral entrance, attached to the

Juv.

NOTES

under surface of palm fronds, banana
leaves, mango clusters, and under fan
palm thatched roofing. Built with fibers
of palms and other plants. *Eggs:* 3-4,
1" x 0.73" (25.4 x 18.5 mm), oval, white
with a bluish-green hue, and brown or
lilac spots toward the broad end.

REFERENCE LOCALITIES:
W **PR:** Sierra de los Órganos, Viñales,
La Güira; **Ar:** Sierra de Anafe; **Mt:**
Ciénaga de Zapata. **C** **Cf:** Topes
de Collantes; **Cm:** Najasa, Sierra de
Cubitas. **E** **Ho:** Mirador de Mayabe,
Cerro de Yaguajay, Gibara: Cupeycillo,
Pinares de Mayarí, Cabonico, Pico
Cristal, Cupeyal, Farallones de Moa;
Gr: Santo Domingo, Cabo Cruz;
SC: Gran Piedra.

♂

Red-shouldered Blackbird
(RSBL)
Agelaius assimilis
Mayito de Ciénaga, Totí de Ciénaga,
Chirriador, Turpial de Hombros
Rojos (SEO)

IDENTIFICATION: 7.5"-9" (19-23 cm).
Overall black with a scarlet red patch
on the shoulders, edged yellow in
the male, absent in female. *Juvenile:*
Reddish-brown patch and overall dull
black. Gregarious behavior. Outside
of the breeding season, usually forms
mixed flocks with Cuban Blackbirds,
Greater Antillean Grackles, and Tawny-
shouldered Blackbirds. Formerly
considered a subspecies of the North
American Red-winged Blackbird
(*A. phoeniceus*), but now separated
based on song differences and the
coloration pattern of females.
GEOGRAPHIC VARIATION: *A. assimilis
assimilis* (Mainland Cuba); *A. a.
subniger* (Isla de la Juventud).

VOICE: Not musical, sort of a
screeching, thus its common name in
Spanish (Chirriador): *Zuiiií fuíu fui
uu-shéc shéc-ti wii uu-owíi uu-owíi iiii
shéc shéc.* While calling, the male lifts
the feathers on its back and shows its
shoulder patches, lowers its wings, and
spreads its tail.
SIMILAR SPECIES: The Tawny-shouldered
Blackbird is more graceful, short bill, tail
forked and rounded at the tip; shoulder
patch is orange with brownish-ochre
tones. Song is different (*shwi shwi shwi
ckwee ckwee twi*). The Cuban Blackbird
is larger, more robust, without color
patches on wings, and has longer bill.
The Shiny Cowbird has no patches on
the wings; has compact bill, purplish
sheen, and more intensely blue plumage.
STATUS, DISTRIBUTION, AND HABITATS:
Vulnerable. Patchy distribution

♂ Juv.

♀

apparently restricted to the western region of Cuba and Isla de la Juventud. Locally common in Ciénaga de Zapata and Guanahacabibes. Occurs in marshes, swamps, and rice fields.

FEEDING: Insects, small fruits, seeds, nectar, small reptiles, and amphibians. It searches for food at outdoor restaurants and consumes kitchen scraps, refuse, and trash (notably in Guamá, Ciénaga de Zapata).

NESTING: April-August. Nest cup-like, made of dry grass, hairs, and feathers, placed close to the ground among tall sawgrass, twigs, or reeds. Occasionally nests in colonies. *Eggs:* 3-4, 0.90" x 0.75" (23 x 17 mm), bluish-white, with brown and pale purple spots.

REFERENCE LOCALITIES:
W **PR:** Lugones, El Jovero, and other lagoons near the road to Guanahacabibes; Playa Guanímar; **IJ:** Ciénaga de Lanier, Cayo Potrero, southern La Vega; **Mt:** Cárdenas and Laguna de Itabo; Ciénaga de Zapata: Laguna del Tesoro, Caleta del Rosario, Caleta del Sábalo, Santo Tomás.

NOTES

_____
_____
_____
_____
_____
_____
_____
_____
_____
_____

Cuban Blackbird (CUBL)
Dives atroviolaceus
Totí, Choncholí, Tordo Cubano (SEO)

IDENTIFICATION: 10"-11" (27-28 cm). Glossy black with blue and purple iridescence. Tail straight, square border. Iris dark. Bill and legs black. Sexes similar. *Juvenile:* Dull black. A common bird in cities and parks throughout Cuba, usually in large flocks; often in mixed flocks with Greater Antillean Grackle, Red-shouldered Blackbird, and Shiny Cowbird, creating a noisy disturbance during the late afternoon while looking for roosts in groves and forests. Observed in pairs during breeding season.

VOICE: Highly varied notes: *Shii u shiiu shii u-shi shi shi wee wee tiií-o tiií-o*, less high-pitched than that of the Greater Antillean Grackle.

SIMILAR SPECIES: The Greater Antillean Grackle has a whitish iris; long, fine bill; and V-shaped tail. The Red-shouldered Blackbird is smaller, less robust, with pointed tail and reddish patch on shoulders, at times not visible, and non-existent in females. The Shiny Cowbird is smaller and has a more conspicuous gloss on its body.

STATUS, DISTRIBUTION, AND HABITATS: Common and widely distributed throughout the mainland, absent from the adjacent cays and Isla de la Juventud. Frequents gardens, rural localities, and cities. Also found in lowland and mountain forests. Moves in flocks searching for food.

FEEDING: Omnivorous, forages around

NOTES

human settlements: ranches, farms, restaurants, and coffee shops, where it ventures inside the facilities to grab food scraps. May be observed perching on cattle, looking for ectoparasites.

NESTING: March-July, mainly April through June. Nest cup-like, among palm fronds, bromeliads, fruit clusters, and in the eaves of roofs. Constructed of dry grass, roots, plant fibers, feathers, hairs, and other soft materials. *Eggs:* 3-4, 1.1"x 0.78" (28.3 x 19.8 mm), grayish-white or greenish-white with highly varied gray and brown dots; oval or elongated oval shape.

REFERENCE LOCALITIES:
Plazas and parks throughout Cuba.

West Indian Whistling-Duck
(*Dendrocygna arborea*)

West Indian Endemics Residing in Cuba

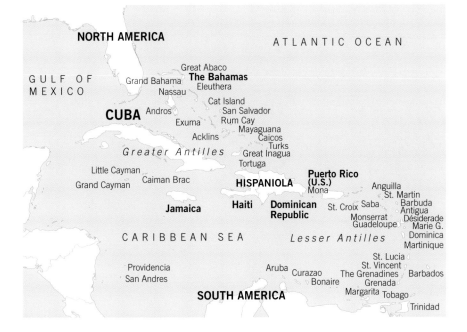

The West Indies comprise three important groups of islands that extend from the eastern tip of the Yucatan peninsula and the southeast of Florida to the coast of Venezuela.

The Bahamas, to the north, form a line in a southeast direction. The Greater Antilles, in the middle, include the islands of Cuba, Hispaniola (Haiti and Dominican Republic), Jamaica, and Puerto Rico. The Lesser Antilles, (Leeward and Windward Islands), which extend to the southeast along the coast of Venezuela, are not included in this book. The total land area of the West Indies comprises 92,541 sq. miles (239,681 km^2); the estimated population is close to 42 million inhabitants.

The entire area as described above contains approximately 564 species of birds; 106 of these are endemic to the region. The illustrations in this chapter show the endemic birds of the West Indies that inhabit the Cuban archipelago; many of them only exist on a few islands. In some cases these birds are rare, endangered or extirpated, consequently they could be classified as near-endemics of Cuba. The Western Spindalis (*Spindalis zena*) and the Thick-billed Vireo (*Vireo crassirostris*) are also included because most of their distribution circumscribes the Greater Antilles and the Bahamas, and only a small nucleus resides on satellite islands of the western Caribbean.

1. West Indian Whistling-Duck (WIWD)
Dendrocygna arbórea
Yaguasa Cubana
→ 9"-22" (48-56 cm). **Vulnerable.**
Locally common. **DISTRIBUTION:** Grand Cayman; Bahamas (Andros, San Salvador, and Inagua islands); Cuba (Cayo Coco); Lesser Antilles (Virgin Islands, Antigua, and Barbuda). Its populations have remained stable in Cuba, while decreasing in the rest of the Caribbean. Nocturnal behavior. **HABITAT:** Dams, reservoirs, and wetlands throughout Cuba.

2. Plain Pigeon (PLPI)
Patagioenas inornata
Torcaza Boba
→ 15"-16" (38-40 cm). **Near threatened.** Uncommon. **DISTRIBUTION:** Endemic to the Greater Antilles: Hispaniola (especially in Dominican Republic); local in Cuba, Jamaica, and Puerto Rico. Its populations have decreased substantially. **HABITAT:** Mainly savannas with palms, lowland forests, and open areas.

3. Cuban Parrot, Rose-throated Parrot, Cuban Amazon (CPAT)
Amazona leucocephala
Perico, Amazona Cubana (SEO)
Cotorra
→ 11"-13" (28-33 cm). **Near threatened.** Locally common. **DISTRIBUTION:** Cuba and Isla de la Juventud; Bahamas (Inagua and Abaco); Cayman Islands (Cayman Brac and Grand Cayman). As a result of conservation efforts, its populations have increased throughout most of its distribution. **HABITAT:** Natural forests and savannas with palms. **ENDEMIC SUBSPECIES:** *A. l. leucocephala* (Central and eastern Cuba).

4. Great Lizard-Cuckoo or Giant Lizard-Cuckoo (GLCU)
Coccyzus merlini
Arriero
→ 17"- 22" (44-55 cm). **Common.** **DISTRIBUTION:** Cuba and Isla de la Juventud; Bahamas. **HABITAT:** All types of forest, from sea level to the mountains. Occasionally found in dense shrubby vegetation, especially close to forests. **ENDEMIC SUBSPECIES:** *C. m. merlini* (Cuba and Cayo Conuco); *C. m. decolor* (Isla de la Juventud); *C. m. santamariae* (Cayo Santamaría and Cayo Coco, north of Camagüey).

5. Antillean Palm Swift (ANPS)
Tachornis phoenicobia
Vencejito de Palma
→ 4"-4.25" (10-11.4 cm). **Common.** **DISTRIBUTION:** Cuba and Isla de la Juventud; Jamaica; Hispaniola (including Isla Saona, Isla Beata, and Île-à-Vache); accidental in Puerto Rico. **HABITAT:** Mainly low and open zones, savannas with palms, sugarcane plantations, cities, suburban and agricultural zones. **ENDEMIC SUBSPECIES:** *T. p. iradii.*

6. Cuban Emerald (CUEM)
Chlorostilbon ricordii
Zunzún
→ 3.5"-4"(9-10.5 cm). **Common.** **DISTRIBUTION:** Cuba and Bahamas. **HABITAT:** All types of natural, secondary, and garden vegetation, from cays at sea

4 Juv.

1

2

3

5

♂ ♀

Juv.

6

level to the mountains. It is the largest and most common of the three species of hummingbirds occurring in Cuba. **ENDEMIC SUBSPECIES:** *C. r.ricordii.*

7. West Indian Woodpecker (WIWO)

Melanerpes superciliaris
Carpintero Jabado (Jabao)
→ 10"-11" (26-28 cm). **Common.**
DISTRIBUTION: Cuba; Bahamas (apparently extirpated from Grand Bahama); Grand Cayman. **HABITAT:** Open areas and forests with abundance of palms and coconut palm groves, agricultural zones, and mangroves.
ENDEMIC SUBSPECIES: *M. s. superciliaris* (Cuba, Cayo Cantiles, Cayo Coco); *M. s. murceus* (Isla de la Juventud); *M. s. florentinoi* (Cayo Largo); *M. s. sanfelipensis* (Cayo Real in the San Felipe Cays), showing some color variations.

8. Crescent-eyed Pewee or Cuban Pewee (CUPE)

Contopus caribaeus
Bobito Chico
→ 5.75"-6.5"(15-16.5 cm). **Common.**
DISTRIBUTION: Cuba; northeastern Bahamas (Grand Bahama, New Providence, Abaco, Andros, Eleuthera, and Cat Island). **HABITAT:** Mangroves, pine groves, natural and secondary forested areas, shrubby vegetation with some trees or tall emerging shrubs.
ENDEMIC SUBSPECIES: *C. c. caribaeus* (Cuba, Isla de la Juventud, Cayo Coco, Cayo Paredón Grande); *C. c. morenoi* (Zapata peninsula and Canarreos archipelago); *C. c. nerlyi* (Jardines de la Reina archipelago); *C. c. florentinoi*

(Jardines de la Reina archipelago); *C. c. sanfelipensis* (San Felipe cays).

9. La Sagra's Flycatcher (LASF)

Myarchus sagrae
Bobito Grande
→ 7.5"-8.5" (19-22 cm). **Common.**
DISTRIBUTION: Cuba and Isla de la Juventud; Bahamas; Grand Cayman.
HABITAT: Mangroves, pine groves, and all forests, from sea level to the mountains.

10. Loggerhead Kingbird (LOKI)

Tyrannus caudifasciatus
Pitirre Guatíbere
→ 9.5"-10" (24-26 cm). **Common.**
DISTRIBUTION: Cuba (Sabana-Camagüey cays, Jardines de la Reina) and Isla de la Juventud; Bahamas (Grand Bahama, Abaco, Andros, New Providence); Jamaica and Cayman Islands. **HABITAT:** Forests and shrubby vegetation with predominance of trees, coffee plantations, mangroves, secondary and managed forest vegetation. **ENDEMIC SUBSPECIES:** *T. c. caudifasciatus.*

11. Giant Kingbird (GIKI)

Tyrannus cubensis
Pitirre Real
→ 9"-10.25" (23-26 cm). **Threatened.** Rare but locally common in some areas. **DISTRIBUTION:** Cuba and Isla de la Juventud. Formerly in the Bahamas (Grand Inagua, Caicos), and while the status of the populations on these islands is unknown at present, it has probably been extirpated. **HABITAT:** Forests close to rivers and marshes, dry savannas with Ceiba trees, mixed

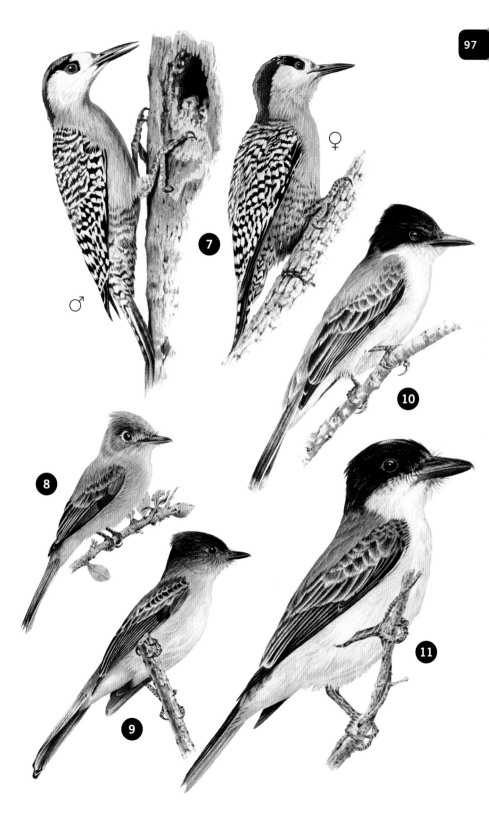

pine groves, natural and semi-natural forest areas with tall trees.

12. Thick-billed Vireo (TBVI)
Vireo crassirostris
Vireo de las Bahamas
→ 5.5" (14 cm). **Locally common.** DISTRIBUTION: Cuba (Cayo Paredón Grande and Cayo Coco. One account on Cayo Romano. After Hurricane Isidore (2002), one individual was captured in Cabo Corrientes, Guanahacabibes peninsula). Bahamas; Cayman Islands; Tortue Island (Hispaniola); and Providencia and Santa Catalina isles in the western Caribbean. HABITAT: Coastal vegetation. ENDEMIC SUBSPECIES: *V. c. cubensis.*

13. Palm Crow (PACR)
Corvus palmarum
Cao Pinalero
→ 17" (43 cm). **Vulnerable.** DISTRIBUTION: Hispaniola; Cuba (locally common in Sierra de Najasa, Tayabito, Miguel, El Jardín and an area called "La 23" near the city of Trinidad. There are no recent reports in the western part around Mina Dora in the Pinar del Río province). HÁBITAT: Forests near pine tree stands and palm groves. Unlike the Cuban Crow, it is accustomed to landing on the ground. ENDEMIC SUBSPECIES: *C. p. minutus.*

14. Cuban Crow (CUCR)
Corvus nasicus
Cao Montero
→ 17.5"- 19" (45-48 cm). **Locally common.** DISTRIBUTION: Cuba, Isla de la Juventud, and the larger cays north of Camagüey and Ciego de Ávila; Caicos Islands. HABITAT: Occurs in forests with open areas, palm groves, and around the edges of marshes.

15. Red-legged Thrush (RLTH)
Turdus plumbeus
Zorzal Real
→ 10"-11" (25-28 cm). **Common.** DISTRIBUTION: Cuba and Isla de la Juventud; northeastern Bahamas (Grand Bahama, Abaco, Andros, New Providence, and Cat Island); Hispaniola (including Gonâve, Tortue, Saona islands); Puerto Rico; Cayman Islands (Cayman Brac); Dominica; Swan Islands. HABITAT: All types of forests and natural or semi-natural shrubby vegetation, plantations and cities, from sea level to the mountains. ENDEMIC SUBSPECIES: *T. p. shistacea* (eastern Cuba).

16. Bahama Mockingbird (BAMO)
Mimus gundlachi
Sinsonte Prieto
→ 11" (28 cm). **Rare.** DISTRIBUTION: Cays of northeastern Cuba; Bahamas; northeastern Jamaica. HABITAT: Semi-arid shrubby vegetation close to the coast, and natural and secondary forested areas.

13

12

14

15
T. p. shistacea
Eastern

15 Juv.

16

15
T. p. rubripes
Western

17. Olive-capped Warbler (OLCW)
Sethophaga pityophila
Bijirita del Pinar
→ 5" (13 cm). **Locally common.**
DISTRIBUTION: Cuba; Bahamas (Grand Bahama and Abaco). **HABITAT:** Occurs only in pine forests. At times may occur on mixed pine groves, always close to natural or secondary pine groves. Distribution irregular in isolated patches.

18. Western Spindalis (WESP), formerly Stripe-headed Tanager
Spindalis zena
Cabrero
→ 5.75" (15 cm). **Locally common.**
DISTRIBUTION: Cuba and Isla de la Juventud; Bahamas; Cayman Islands (Grand Cayman); Cozumel. **HABITAT:** All types of vegetation, mainly natural forests, from sea level to mountains.
ENDEMIC SUBSPECIES: *S. z. pretrei* (mainland Cuba; Isla de la Juventud; Cantiles, Francés, and Santa María cays).

19. Cuban Bullfinch (CUBU)
Melopyrrha nigra
Negrito
→ 5.5"-5.75" (14-15 cm). **Locally common**, but its populations have declined in recent years due to capture as a caged bird. Recent studies suggest that the Cuban populations differ at the specific level from those of the Cayman Islands. **DISTRIBUTION:** Cuba; Isla de la Juventud; some northeastern cays and Cayo Cantiles to the south of Cuba; Grand Cayman. **HABITAT:** Forests, pine groves, mangroves, thickets, natural and secondary shrubby vegetation from sea level to

mountains. **ENDEMIC SUBSPECIES:** *M. n. nigra.*

20. Greater Antillean Grackle (GAGR)
Quiscalus niger
Chichinguaco
→ 10"-12" (25-30 cm). **Common.**
DISTRIBUTION: Cuba and cays adjacent to Isla de la Juventud; Jamaica; Hispaniola (Gonave, Tortue, Beata, Île-à-Vache); Puerto Rico (including Isla de Vieques); Cayman Islands except Cayman Brac; introduced to the Virgin Islands (St. Croix). **HABITAT:** Forests and open areas, gardens, pasture lands, agricultural areas, urban and rural zones, marshes and mangroves.
ENDEMIC SUBSPECIES: *Q. n. gundlachi*; (Cuba, with the exception of the extreme western part, Cayo Coco, Cayo Romano, Cayo Guajaba and others); *Q. n. caribaeus* (Cabo de San Antonio and Isla de la Juventud).

21. Tawny-shouldered Blackbird (TSBL)
Agelaius humeralis
Mayito de Cantiles
→ 7.5"-8.5" (19-22 cm). **Common.**
DISTRIBUTION: Cuba, Isla de la Juventud, and Cuban cays; Hispaniola (Haiti).
HABITAT: Natural and cultivated forests, gardens, groves in urban and rural parks, pasture lands, rice fields, marshes. **ENDEMIC SUBSPECIES:** *A. h. scopulus* (Cayo Cantiles, Cuba).

20 ♂

Eastern

Western

17

Juv.

18 ♀

20 ♀

18 ♂

19 ♂

19 *Juv.*

21 ♂

19 ♀

21 ♂ *Juv.*

21 ♀

Semi-deciduous forest on karst in Ciénaga de Zapata

3
Habitats

Along with the morphological characteristics distinct to each species, the habitats where they occur also have particularities and are generally a good indicator as to the whereabouts of either one or several species. They are the basis for protecting any endangered animal.

The first step in finding a bird in Cuba is to know its distribution and preferred habitat. For instance, it would be difficult to find the Cuban Solitaire in shrubby formations in low-lying areas, but one could possibly spot it in little-disturbed forests in the mountains. Likewise, look for an Eastern Meadowlark in savannas, never in the forest.

Knowledge of habitat is also a tool that will help differentiate between very similar birds, such as the Blue-gray and Cuban Gnatcatchers. The habitats of Cuban land birds may be characterized in terms of vegetative formations. These, although of a wide variety, are grouped in seven types: forests, thickets, herbaceous communities, savannas, vegetation complexes, semi-natural vegetation, and cultivated vegetation, according to the classifications of Cuban vegetation by Capote y Berzain, 1989.

Tropical rain forest

Forests

Arboreal formations. There is a high diversity of forest types in Cuba, which vary in species composition, structure, altitude, and canopy cover. They are found from sea level to the highest mountains. The most common forest formation on the island is the semi-deciduous forest, which develops primarily on limestone terrains and carbonated soils.

TYPES: Semi-deciduous, evergreen, lowland and highland tropical rain forest, mangrove, pine forest, gallery (along rivers), and swamp forest.

BIRD RICHNESS: High.

FREQUENT ENDEMIC BIRDS: Cuban Tody, Cuban Trogon, Cuban Pygmy-Owl, Cuban Green Woodpecker, Cuban Vireo, Bee Hummingbird, Cuban Solitaire, Cuban Oriole, Oriente Warbler, and Yellow-headed Warbler.

Semi-deciduous forest

▲ Swamp forest   ▼ Pine forest

▲ Gallery forest   ▼ Mangroves

Sub-spiny xenomorphic thicket over serpentine rock

Thickets

Low shrubby formations where some isolated trees may occasionally be present. A habitat with predominance of shrubs, generally thorny, spiny and with small leaves. Coastal and sub-coastal xenomorphic thickets are the most frequent types on the island.

TYPES: Subparamo, sub-spiny xenomorphic thicket over serpentine rock (*charrascal*); spiny xenomorphic thicket over serpentine rock (*cuabal*); coastal and subcoastal xenomorphic; subcoastal sclerophyll; coastal spiny semi-desert (characteristic of the southeastern coast of Cuba between Guantánamo and Maisí).

BIRD RICHNESS: Medium to high.

FREQUENT ENDEMIC BIRDS: Cuban Gnatcatcher, Cuban Vireo, Cuban Green Woodpecker, Bee Hummingbird, Cuban Grassquit, Cuban Sparrow (Eastern subspecies), Yellow-headed Warbler, and Oriente Warbler.

Semi-desert spiny hyper-xenomorphic formation

▲ Coastal xenomorphic thicket

▲ Coastal xenomorphic thicket   ▼ Sub-coastal thicket

Savanna

Savannas

Commonly known as grasslands with abundant herbaceous cover, sparse trees and bushes, a few palms, and vines.

TYPES: Semi-natural with different sized palms, pines, deforested areas.

BIRD RICHNESS: Low.

FREQUENT ENDEMIC BIRDS: Red-shouldered Blackbird, Cuban Grassquit and Cuban Blackbird.

▲ Savanna with isolated trees ▼ Savanna with palms

Aquatic vegetation

Grassy communities

Found in freshwater and saltwater marshes and along the banks of streams and rivers. They may cover extensive areas, temporarily or permanently flooded. Characteristic species are: cattail (*Typha dominguensis*); knotted or jointed spikerush (*Eleocharis interstincta*); two-edged sawgrass (*Cladium jamaicensis*) nutsedge (*Cyperus* spp.); sugarcane plumegrass (*Erianthus giganteus*); and fire flag (*Thalia geniculata*), combined with palms of the genera *Coccotrinax* and *Sabal*.

TYPES: Aquatic vegetation along riverbanks and streams, marshy and swampy grassland.

BIRD RICHNESS: High.

FREQUENT ENDEMIC BIRDS: The grasslands in Ciénaga de Zapata are home to some of Cuba's most restricted and threatened endemic species, including Zapata Rail, Zapata Wren, Cuban Sparrow, and Red-shouldered Blackbird.

▲▼ Swampy grasslands

Sandy coastal vegetation

Vegetation complexes

A combination of different plant communities, which, because of their characteristics and distribution, present a unique appearance. These habitats generally do not occupy large areas and are often found only on a small strip of land on coastal edges or on the steep walls of *mogotes* (limestone hills).

TYPES: Mountainous karst; the mountains of Escambray; western and eastern submountainous karst; hummocks; sandy coast; rocky coast.

BIRD RICHNESS: Medium.

FREQUENT ENDEMIC BIRDS: Cuban Green Woodpecker, Gray-fronted Quail-Dove, Cuban Grassquit, Cuban Pygmy Owl, Gundlach's Hawk, Cuban Gnatcatcher, Cuban Vireo, Oriente Warbler, and Yellow-headed Warbler.

▲ Rocky coastal vegetation complex ▼ Sandy coastal vegetation ▲ Mogote vegetation complex

Semi-natural vegetation

Remnant forests and thickets modified by human activities that still retain important elements of their floristic composition. Includes secondary herbaceous communities.

BIRD RICHNESS: Medium-high, varies according to complexity and structure. Related to the edge effect at the boundaries of two habitats.

FREQUENT ENDEMIC BIRDS: Cuban Blackbird, Cuban Grassquit, Cuban Vireo, Cuban Tody, Cuban Pygmy Owl, Gundlach's Hawk, Bee Hummingbird, Greater Antillean Oriole and Cuban Green Woodpecker.

Human-dominated vegetation

Associated with agricultural crops; most importantly with pastures, secondary vegetation, and forest plantations.

BIRD RICHNESS: Low, but varies depending on the vegetation structure. Rice fields and crops associated with wetlands have higher species richness. **FREQUENT ENDEMIC BIRDS:** Cuban Blackbird, Gundlach's Hawk and Cuban Grassquit.

Gundlach's Hawk (*Accipiter gundlachi*)

Birds in their habitats

(Species are listed in a way that facilitates their identification and comparison with similar species, independently of their taxonomy).

Cuban Black Hawk (*Buteogallus gundlachi*)

Gray-fronted Quail-Dove (*Geotrygon caniceps*)

© ERNESTO REYES

Plain Pigeon (*Patagioenas inornata*)

Blue-headed Quail-Dove (*Starnoenas cyanocephala*)

West Indian Whistling-Duck (*Dendrocygna arborea*)

Bare-legged Owl (*Margarobyas lawrencii*)

Cuban Nightjar (*Antrostomus cubanensis*)

Great Lizard-Cuckoo (*Coccyzus merlini*)

Cuban Pygmy Owl (*Glaucidium siju*)

© MAIKEL CAÑIZARES

Cuban Nightjar (*Antrostomus cubanensis*)

Cuban Tody (*Todus multicolor*)

Cuban Emerald (*Chlorostilbon ricordii*)

Cuban Parakeet (*Psittacara euops*)

Cuban Trogon (*Priotelus temnurus*)

Bee Hummingbird (*Mellisuga helenae*)

Cuban Parrot (*Amazona leucocephala*)

Cuban Green Woodpecker (*Xiphidiopicus percussus*)

Fernandina's Flicker (*Colaptes fernandinae*)

West Indian Woodpecker (*Melanerpes superciliaris*)

Antillean Palm Swift (*Tachornis phoenicobia*)

Cuban Crow (*Corvus nasicus*)

Palm Crow (*Corvus palmarum*)

Cuban Pewee (*Contopus caribaeus*)

Loggerhead Kingbird (*Tyrannus caudifasciatus*)

Thick-billed Vireo (*Vireo crassirostris*)

La Sagra's Flycatcher (*Myiarchus sagrae*)

Giant Kingbird (*Tyrannus cubensis*)

Cuban Vireo (*Vireo gundlachi*)

Zapata Wren (*Ferminia cerverai*)

Cuban Gnatcatcher (*Polioptila lembeyei*)

Cuban Sparrow (*Torreornis inexpectata inexpectata*)

Cuban Solitaire (*Myadestes elisabeth*)

© ERNESTO REYES

Bahama Mockingbird (*Mimus gundlachi*)

Cuban Sparrow (*Torreornis inexpectata sigmani*)

Oriente Warbler (*Teretistris forrsi*)

Yellow-headed Warbler (*Teretistris fernandinae*)

Olive-capped Warbler (*Sethophaga pityophila*)

Red-legged Thrush (*Turdus plumbeus*)

Western Spindalis (*Spindalis zena*)

Cuban Grassquit (*Tiaris canorus*)

Tawny-shouldered Blackbird (*Agelaius humeralis*)

Cuban Blackbird (*Dives atroviolaceus*)

Cuban Oriole (*Icterus melanopsis*)

Red-shouldered Blackbird (*Agelaius assimilis*)

Greater Antillean Grackle (*Quiscalus niger*)

Cuban Bullfinch (*Melopyrrha nigra*)

Blue-headed Quail-Dove
(*Starnoenas cyanocephala*)

4

Conservation Status
of Threatened Birds of Cuba

The information presented here about endangered species is based on criteria proposed by the International Union for Conservation of Nature (IUCN) and BirdLife International (2014) in their list of globally threatened species. Additional data comes from the *Libro Rojo de los Vertebrados de Cuba* (2012) (Red Data Book), the Convention on International Trade in Endangered Species of Wild Fauna and Flora (CITES), and is updated with recent field surveys.

The main threats to Cuban birds are progressive habitat loss from logging, mining, tourism, and drainage of wetlands for conversion to agricultural use. Illegal hunting for food has affected some medium-sized birds, such as pigeons and ducks. The capture and traffic of wild birds for caged pets is an additional threat, as is predation by feral animals. Laws punishing anyone who harms or collects animals and plants illegally were put into practice in the year 2000 with Decree No. 200, which describes infractions and fines; however their application is currently insufficient (*see page 146*).

National experts, in unison with the Red Data Book, have proposed additions and changes to the categories of threat, classifying as **Vulnerable**: Masked Duck (*Nomonyx dominicus*); Sandhill Crane (*Grus canadensis*); Snowy Plover (*Charadrius nivosus*); Roseate Tern (*Sterna dougallii*); Thick-billed Vireo (*Vireo crassirostris*); Olive-capped Warbler (*Setophaga pityophila*); Red-shouldered Blackbird (*Agelaius assimilis*); **Near Threatened**: Bahama Mockingbird (*Mimus gundlachi*); Cuban Bullfinch (*Melopyrrha nigra*).

All threatened species in Cuba are listed here (*see* Classification of Threatened Species, *next page*), but only the Cuban and West Indian endemics that occur in the geographic area covered by this guidebook are described in this chapter.

Levels of endemism are referred to in the following way:

• **WEST INDIES:** Covers the majority of islands in the Atlantic and the Caribbean, including the Bahamas and the Greater and Lesser Antilles.

• **CARIBBEAN:** Only the islands in the Caribbean basin (Greater and Lesser Antilles, does not include the Bahamas).

• **GREATER ANTILLES:** Includes Cuba, Cayman Islands, Jamaica, Hispaniola, and Puerto Rico.

When a species is resident in Cuba and another island or isolated group of islands, the name of each location is noted.

Threatened Species in Cuba

Common Name	Cuban Common Name	Scientific Name	IUCN Code
Black-Capped Petrel	Pájaro de las Brujas	*Pterodroma hasitata*	EN
Sooty Shearwater	Pampero Oscuro	*Puffinus griseus*	NT
West Indian Whistling-duck	Yaguasa	*Dendrocygna arborea*	VU
Cuban Kite	Gavilán Caguarero	*Chondrohierax wilsonii*	CR
Gundlach's Hawk	Gavilán Colilargo	*Accipiter gundlachi*	EN
Cuban Black Hawk	Gavilán Batista	*Buteogallus gundlachi*	NT
Northern Bobwhite	Codorniz	*Colinus virginianus*	NT
Black Rail	Gallinuela Oscura	*Laterallus jamaicensis*	NT
Zapata Rail	Gallinuela de Santo Tomás	*Cyanolimnas cerverai*	CR
Caribbean Coot	Gallareta del Caribe	*Fulica caribaea*	NT
Piping Plover	Frailecillo Silvador	*Charadrius melodus*	NT
Buff-breasted Sandpiper	Zarapico Piquicorto	*Tryngites subruficollis*	NT
White-crowned Pigeon	Torcaza Cabeciblanca	*Columba leucocephala*	EN
Plain Pigeon	Torcaza Boba	*Columba inornata*	NT
Blue-headed Quail-dove	Paloma Perdiz	*Starnoenas cyanocephala*	EN
Gray-headed Quail-dove	Camao	*Geotrygon caniceps*	VU
Cuban Macaw	Guacamayo Cubano	*Ara tricolor*	EX
Cuban Parakeet	Catey	*Psittacara euops*	VU
Cuban Parrot	Cotorra	*Amazona leucocephla*	NT
Bee Hummingbird	Zunzuncito	*Mellisuga helenae*	NT
Fernandina's Flicker	Carpintero Churroso	*Colaptes fernandinae*	VU
Ivory-billed Woodpecker	Carpintero Real	*Campephilus principalis*	CR
Giant Kingbird	Pitirre Real	*Tyrannus cubensis*	EN
Zapata Wren	Ferminia	*Ferminia cerverai*	EN
Cuban Solitaire	Ruiseñor	*Myadestes elisabeth*	NT
Bicknell's Thrush	Tordo de Bicknell	*Catharus bicknelli*	VU
Cuban Sparrow	Cabrerito de la Ciénaga	*Torreornis inexpectata*	EN
Painted Bunting	Pájaro Mariposa	*Passerina ciris*	NT
Bachman's Warbler	Bijirita de Bachman	*Vermivora bachmanii*	CR
Golden-winged Warbler	Bijirita Alidorada	*Vermivora chrysoptera*	NT
Cerulean Warbler	Bijirita Azulada	*Dendroica cerulea*	VU
Palm Crow	Cao Pinalero	*Corvus palmarum*	NT

CRITICALLY ENDANGERED

Cuban Kite

Gavilán Caguarero (*Chondrohierax wilsonii*)

→ This species, previously treated as a subspecies of *C. uncinatus*, has suffered a drastic reduction in numbers and range, and now has an extremely limited population, restricted to just one small area. It is in danger of imminent extinction. **Critically Endangered**.

POPULATION ESTIMATE: 50-249

POPULATION TREND: Decreasing

ESTIMATED AREA: 1,506 sq. miles (3,900 km²)

ENDEMISM LEVEL: Cuba

THREATS: Its reduction has been attributed mainly to the destruction and alteration of its habitats caused by the cutting of forests and their conversion to agricultural lands, mining, and local customs. Farmers kill this species under the erroneous belief that the Kite feeds on their poultry. In addition, land snails, an essential food for the Kite, have become scarce due to agricultural practices and indiscriminate collecting to sell to tourists.

CONSERVATION MEASURES ADOPTED: CITES Appendix II. The current area of distribution is within a large protected area: Alejandro de Humboldt National Park, where community campaigns have helped to raise awareness with the local populations on the importance of protecting this species.

CONSERVATION MEASURES PROPOSED: Conduct expeditions to areas where the bird was reported and photographed in 2004 and 2009. Clarify the population numbers and distribution. Establish effective protection of the Kite habitats and of land snails. Develop awareness and public education campaigns to reduce persecution. Protect the species under Cuban laws and designate the localities of the most recent sightings as protected areas.

Zapata Rail

Gallinuela de Santo Tomás (*Cyanolimnas cerverai*)

→ The species qualifies as **Critically Endangered** because the two known populations are restricted to only one area, Ciénaga de Zapata, where habitat loss and depredation have affected population size and distribution.

POPULATION ESTIMATE: 250-999

POPULATION TREND: Decreasing

ESTIMATED AREA: 77 sq. miles (200 km²)

ENDEMISM LEVEL: Cuba

THREATS: Initially the extensive cutting of grass for thatching roofs, together with devastating dry season fires, affected natural habitats. Exotic species such as mongooses and rats are likely important predators. The introduction of the highly voracious, resilient, and rapidly increasing African sharptooth catfish in 1999-2000 presents a threat to the Rail. The adverse impact caused by this fish, which is capable of eating land species, is considered to be very high, although there are no known studies on the matter.

CONSERVATION MEASURES ADOPTED: Both populations are within a protected area of Ciénaga de Zapata:

Corral de Santo Tomás Wildlife Refuge, and a tourism natural zone that includes the Laguna del Tesoro. Monitoring of its distribution was conducted in 1998 with unsatisfactory results.

CONSERVATION MEASURES PROPOSED: Carry out expeditions to locate the species and conduct studies to define its seasonal distribution, status, and ecology. Control fires during the dry season. Investigate new possibilities for habitat management and recommend future strategies. Determine the impact of the African sharptooth catfish on the ecosystems in the area of distribution.

ENDANGERED

Gundlach's Hawk

Gavilán Colilargo (*Accipiter gundlachi*) → The species is classified as **Endangered** on the basis of its small and seriously fragmented populations that are substantially decreasing.

POPULATION ESTIMATE: Fewer than 2,500

POPULATION TREND: Decreasing

ESTIMATED AREA: 14,000 sq. miles (22,620 km²)

ENDEMISM LEVEL: Cuba

THREATS: Habitat loss, habitat conversion to agricultural lands; killing by humans because of their poultry depredation. Habitat has diminished 80% in the last 100 years, leaving a fragmented population where no nucleus reaches 250 mature individuals. Potential distribution would only be 22% of its original distribution, with less than half of that in 22 of the protected areas of Cuba.

CONSERVATION MEASURES ADOPTED: CITES Appendix II. Personnel from Sierra Maestra, Sierra Cristal, and Humboldt National Parks have initiated education programs for the communities living in and near the parks, but currently these are on a very small scale.

CONSERVATION MEASURES PROPOSED: Monitor Pinar del Río and Ciénaga de Zapata colonies; continue to determine the status and trends of the present populations in areas of eastern Cuba. Define the species' ecological requirements. Conduct public education and awareness campaigns to emphasize the difficult situation of the species and to dissuade people from killing it.

Blue-headed Quail-Dove

Paloma Perdiz (*Starnoenas cyanocephala*) → Extremely rare, found in small populations, in numbers that are substantially and rapidly diminishing. This combination qualifies the species as **Endangered**.

POPULATION ESTIMATE: 1,000-2,499

POPULATION TREND: Decreasing

ESTIMATED AREA: 11,043 sq. miles (28,600 km²)

ENDEMISM LEVEL: Cuba

THREATS: Combined effects of excessive hunting and habitat destruction have caused its large-scale reduction. Quail-Doves are illegally hunted with traps because they are considered a delicacy. Hurricanes may significantly affect this species because of the extensive loss of trees in large tracts of forests, as in the case of Ciénaga de Zapata in 1996. Studies conducted in the 1990s found the population density of this dove low and fluctuating between 2 and 20 birds per acre (5-40 birds/hectar).

CONSERVATION MEASURES ADOPTED: Protected under national laws in Ciénaga de Zapata; however, these laws are not often enforced and the hunting continues. The Quail-Dove is found in nine protected areas of the country. The only protected populations in mountainous zones are within La Güira National Park and Viñales National Park.

CONSERVATION MEASURES PROPOSED: Monitor areas outside Ciénaga de Zapata and La Güira, where the species may persist. Ensure immediate protection of the populations discovered. Carry out public education and awareness campaigns on the risks to this species in an effort to alleviate pressure on it. Captive breeding programs and reintroduction of the species could help to increase the wild populations.

Giant Kingbird

Pitirre Real (*Tyrannus cubensis*)
→ Rapid decrease in numbers for unknown reasons. The Giant Kingbird is considered to be extirpated in two of the three island groups where it formerly occurred (Gran Inagua and Caicos). It is classified as **Endangered** because of its small population and severely fragmented distribution that continues to decrease substantially.

POPULATION ESTIMATE: 250-999
POPULATION TREND: Decreasing
ESTIMATED AREA: 428 sq. miles (1,110 km²)

ENDEMISM LEVEL: Cuba, Isla de la Juventud, and the Bahamas (recently only occuring in Cuba).

THREATS: The reasons for the decrease of this species have not been determined, but habitat loss and felling of trees for agriculture are probably the most important factors.

CONSERVATION MEASURES ADOPTED: Found in four protected areas in the country. A study of its breeding ecology was carried out at Sierra de Najasa, and surveys of the eastern population were conducted in 2008.

CONSERVATION MEASURES PROPOSED: Monitor distribution, especially in areas around Moa and Gibara, where it is apparently extirpated, as well as other historic sites in Pinar del Río, including the Guanahacabibes Peninsula. Follow up on the Sierra de Najasa project and carry out new efforts to define its ecological requirements. Protect the remaining habitats where it still survives.

Zapata Wren

Ferminia (*Ferminia cerverai*)
→ Because of its highly restricted distribution and reduced population size, which is limited to one area and continues to decrease, it is classified as **Endangered**. Population estimate: 1,000-2,499 (Could be as low as 250 individuals per nucleus).

POPULATION TREND: Decreasing. Abundance within populations is low with a patchy distribution located in only one region of Cuba (Ciénaga de Zapata).

ESTIMATED AREA: 232 sq. miles (600 km²)
ENDEMISM LEVEL: Cuba

THREATS: Fires during droughts and the draining of wetlands for agricultural purposes destroy and degrade the appropriate habitats. Depredation by rats, mongooses, and African sharptooth catfish are also a potential problem.

CONSERVATION MEASURES ADOPTED: The Wren habitat in Ciénaga de Zapata has protected area status, but regulations are poorly enforced. Monitoring programs were conducted in 1998 and more recently in 2011 and 2012.

CONSERVATION MEASURES PROPOSED: New surveys to accurately determine its distribution, population size, and threats.

Cuban Sparrow or Zapata Sparrow

Cabrerito de la Ciénaga (*Torreornis inexpectata*)

→ Restricted to only three geographically distinct areas: Ciénaga de Zapata, Cayo Coco, and the southern coast of Guantánamo. Habitat loss continues in its limited range, and in the latter two of these areas it is apparently decreasing in numbers. Population density is low. **Endangered**.

POPULATION ESTIMATE: 1,000-2,499

POPULATION TREND: Decreasing

ESTIMATED AREA: 722 sq. miles (1,870 km²)

ENDEMISM LEVEL: Cuba

THREATS: Drainage and fires during the dry season affect the habitat in Ciénaga de Zapata. Cayo Coco is a tourism development area. Slash and burn of habitats, with the subsequent invasion of grasses, and fencing for sheep threaten the population on the southern coast of Guantánamo. The Cuban Sparrow has been sighted in 17 localities of three regions in Cuba, where its habitat is fragmented and has diminished 20% in 20 years.

CONSERVATION MEASURES ADOPTED: Even though each of the three subspecies occurs within a protected area, none of them receives special protection. Surveys funded by British Birdwatching Fair of the eastern subspecies have contributed to a better understanding of the species.

CONSERVATION MEASURES PROPOSED: Conduct studies to define the range of each subspecies. Secure a level of protection that is geared toward conservation at each of the reserves. Investigate possible development plans and take mitigation measures in each site. Develop a scheme whereby farming and conservation of the species are compatible.

VULNERABLE

West Indian Whistling-Duck

Yaguasa (*Dendrocygna arborea*)

→ The species has been classified as **Vulnerable** because populations throughout its range are small and severely fragmented. Furthermore, the quality of habitats has undergone a substantial reduction; this species has disappeared from some sites. However, there is evidence that the West Indian Whistling-Duck may now be increasing in some areas where rice growing and land flooding techniques have improved.

POPULATION ESTIMATE: 10,000-19,999. In Cuba estimates are about 14,000 individuals.

POPULATION TREND: Decreasing
ESTIMATED AREA: 9,228 sq. miles
(23,900 km²). In Cuba 772 sq. miles
(2,000 km²)
ENDEMISM LEVEL: West Indies
THREATS: Excessive and non-regulated
hunting for food (including eggs)
has been the basic cause of its
population decrease. Wetlands are
limited habitats in the Caribbean,
highly susceptible to conversion to
agricultural lands and other uses.
More than 50% of the existing
wetlands are seriously degraded
from destruction of mangroves and
swamp forests, pollution (especially
pesticides), and natural catastrophes
such as droughts and hurricanes.
Predation is not properly documented
but is probably a relevant factor. In
Cuba (Granma province), there have
been reports of illegal hunting with
the use of pesticides by unscrupulous
people who then sell the meat for
human consumption. In spite of
continued calls of alarm from the
Cuban Federation of Sports Hunters,
no steps have been taken to prevent
these crimes.
CONSERVATION MEASURES ADOPTED:
CITES Appendix II. CMS Appendix II.
Legally protected throughout its range,
but law enforcement is inadequate.
The "West Indian Whistling-Duck
Working Group" of BirdsCaribbean
initiated a successful conservation
program in 1997. Although there are
many protected areas in the region,
wetlands are poorly represented.
CONSERVATION MEASURES PROPOSED:
Assess population numbers and
distribution. Help local authorities in
establishing long-term monitoring

programs. Conserve key sites. Initiate
environmental education campaigns
geared at raising public awareness,
especially with members of the Cuban
Hunters Federation. Determine
protocols for captive breeding
programs for the *ex situ* conservation
of the species.

Gray-fronted Quail-Dove
Camao (*Geotrygon caniceps*)
→ The population is reduced: classified
as **Vulnerable**.
POPULATION ESTIMATE: 2,500-9,999
POPULATION TREND: Decreasing
ESTIMATED AREA: 10,811 sq. miles
(28,000 km²)
ENDEMISM LEVEL: Cuba
THREATS: The expansion of cacao,
coffee, and tobacco plantations
perceptibly threatens the available
habitats. Fires during droughts,
drainage, and agricultural expansion
are severe problems in Ciénaga de
Zapata and other localities. Predation
of eggs and nests by introduced
species such as rats, dogs, cats, pigs
and mangooses is a potential threat for
the survival of this species. The Quail-
Dove is hunted for food using traps
with orange seeds as bait.
CONSERVATION MEASURES ADOPTED:
Occurs in several protected areas
(Ciénaga de Zapata, La Güira, Sierra
del Rosario, and Sierra de Nipe),
however, it has received very little
effective protection. Studies conducted
in one of the localities with the highest
abundance of species showed a density
of only 0.15 to 0.35 birds per acre
(0.31-0.70 birds/hectar).
CONSERVATION MEASURES PROPOSED:
Monitor the present status of the

species and determine the protected areas where they occur. Implement management programs for protected areas. Captive breeding programs could help to increase the wild populations in some areas.

Cuban Parakeet
Catey (*Psittacara euops*)
→ The species has declined rapidly and now has a small, fragmented range. **Vulnerable.** The Red Data Book proposes a change in level of threat to **Threatened** because of its fragmented populations and diminished habitat (down 20% in the last 50 years).

POPULATION ESTIMATE: 1,300-2,000 individuals
POPULATION TREND: Decreasing
ESTIMATED AREA: 4,595 sq. miles (11,900 km²)
ENDEMISM LEVEL: Cuba
THREATS: Capture for the pet trade, as well as habitat loss. Gregarious habits during the nesting period make the Parakeet more susceptible to capture. A significant threat is the loss of nests as a result of hurricanes (e.g., Lili in Ciénaga de Zapata, 1996) and the cutting of trees in search of Rose-throated Parrot fledglings (*Amazona leucocephala*).

CONSERVATION MEASURES ADOPTED:
CITES Appendix II. Legally protected. There are recognized populations in 16 protected areas of Cuba. The species occurs at seven natural reserves, including Zapata and Birama swamps and Pico Cristal. Research, together with an intensive public education campaign, has helped to establish an effective management program. Population and reproduction studies are being conducted on the central and eastern populations in Banao, Pico San Juan, and Ciénaga de Birama.

CONSERVATION MEASURES PROPOSED:
Conduct further research to determine the ecological requirements of the parakeet. Conserve additional habitats, especially nesting areas. Develop conservation measures in its breeding areas. Continue reintroduction of the species to Isla de la Juventud. Develop protocols for captive breeding and *ex situ* conservation programs combined with the reintroduction to localities where it has existed in the past. Improve measures to punish those involved in the illegal trade of both species of Psittacidae in Cuba.

Fernandina's Flicker
Carpintero Churroso (*Colaptes fernandinae*)
The species has been classified as **Vulnerable** because of its drastically and rapidly reduced population size, which is severely fragmented: approximately 50% of its habitats have shrunk in the past 40 years.

POPULATION ESTIMATE: 600-800. The largest subpopulation occurs in Ciénaga de Zapata and is estimated at no more than 250 individuals. The remaining populations are small and do not exceed 20 or 30 mature individuals, most of which are located outside of protected areas.
POPULATION TREND: Decreasing
ESTIMATED AREA: 2,857 sq. miles (7,400 km²)
ENDEMISM LEVEL: Cuba
THREATS: The felling of trees for

agricultural conversion is the main threat. The Flicker often shares nesting trees with the Cuban Parrot. Poachers sometimes cut down these trees to steal parrot chicks; but this affects both species and causes permanent loss of the breeding habitat. Hurricanes have a devastating effect on dead palms, as was evidenced in Bermejas after Hurricane Lili in 1996. The West Indian Woodpecker (*Melanerpes superciliaris*) has been known to depredate Flicker eggs and nestlings.

CONSERVATION MEASURES ADOPTED: The extensive Ciénaga de Zapata is a natural reserve; however, there are not enough park guards to patrol the area. The populations of Ciénaga de Birama are protected within a fauna refuge and that population is monitored during the breeding season. Populations have been found in only seven protected areas.

CONSERVATION MEASURES PROPOSED: Design and distribute posters in towns in the vicinity of Ciénaga de Zapata to raise awareness on the importance and vulnerability of this species and others, such as the Cuban Parrot (*Amazona leucocephala*). Mount artificial nests in palms within and around the nesting areas. Reduce the felling of nest trees. Conduct expeditions to register unknown populations, and establish the status of populations like that of Gibara, where it is assumed to be extirpated.

Thick-billed Vireo

Vireo de las Bahamas (*Vireo crassirostris*)
→ The Red Data Book classifies the population of the archipelago

Vulnerable because it is an endemic subspecies of Cuba's northern cays.

POPULATION ESTIMATE IN CUBA: Unknown

POPULATION TREND IN CUBA: Decreasing

ESTIMATED AREA IN CUBA: 40 sq. miles (100 km²)

ENDEMISM LEVEL: Cuba, Bahamas

THREATS IN CUBA: Limited to only three localities: Cayo Paredón Grande, Cayo Coco, and Cayo Romano. The first two habitats are threatened because of the development of tourism. Other serious threats are the transformation, reduction, and fragmentation of habitats. All Cuban populations are threatened.

CONSERVATION MEASURES ADOPTED: The three localities are within protected areas; no other specific measures for conservation of this species are known.

CONSERVATION MEASURES PROPOSED: Determine the extent of the area where the species is present in Cuba, in particular, its status in Guanahacabibes. Conserve habitats and monitor the species in zones affected by toursim.

Red-shouldered Blackbird

Mayito de Ciénaga (*Agelaius assimilis*)
→ The Cuban populations were formerly considered part of the form *phoeniceus*, which is amply distributed. In 1996, it was determined to be a separate species, and became a Cuban endemic. Its populations are very fragmented and restricted to a few localities: Laguna de Lugones in Guanahacabibes, Ciénaga de Lanier on Isla de la Juventud, Ciénaga de Zapata, and Ciénaga de Majaguillar

north of Matanzas. Because of its limited distribution and association with fragile ecosystems, the species is classified as **Vulnerable**.

POPULATION ESTIMATE: Unknown but quite small

POPULATION TREND: Decreasing

ESTIMATED AREA: 155 sq. miles (400 km²)

ENDEMISM LEVEL: Cuba

THREATS: Limited distribution and association with fragile ecosystems in fresh water wetlands, as well as impacts from anthropization and climatic phenomena. Intensive use of water, excesive dry spells, spontaneous forest fires and those caused by illegal hunters of crocodiles and turtles.

CONSERVATION METHODS ADOPTED: Two of the four localities are outside protected areas. No conservation practices are known.

CONSERVATION METHODS PROPOSED: Work with habitat management; determine the true range of distribution; conduct environmental education programs, especially with the communities near and in their habitats. Confirm the species' existence in less studied areas through careful monitoring.

Olive-capped Warbler

Bijirita del Pinar (*Setophaga pityophila*)

→ In spite of the fact that it has not received an official designation of threat from the IUCN, the Red Data Book proposes classifying this species **Vulnerable** within Cuban territory. Its regional distribution is reduced, and the Cuban populations are limited to the western and eastern part of the island. The pine forests where they live have been intensely modified because of mining and harvesting trees for wood. In the eastern region alone, between 50 and 60% of the habitats have been lost and only 10% of those remaining are in protected areas. One of the largest populations is in Pinares de Mayarí in Sierra de Nipe, where 75% of the endemic pine (*Pinus cubensis*) forest has disappeared, restricting the habitat to only 25,000 acres. The other pine forests in the country are exploited for wood and so rotated every 15 years.

No other options exist for the protection of the species in other areas because of a lack of appropriate habitats.

POPULATION ESTIMATE IN CUBA: Unknown

POPULATION TENDENCY: Decreasing in Cuba

ESTIMATED AREA IN CUBA: 193 sq. miles (500 km²)

ENDEMISM LEVEL: Cuba, Bahamas

THREATS: Intense modification, reduction, and fragmentation of habitat because of exploitation of forests and mining. The bird has a limited range of distribution regionally, and a scarcity of habitats which are frequently affected by severe storms and hurricanes.

CONSERVATION METHODS ADOPTED: The species is found in four protected areas, but there are currently no special efforts at conservation.

CONSERVATION METHODS PROPOSED: Emphasize programs designed for conservation of specific forested and mining areas. Determine the taxonomic status of the eastern and western populations in Cuba.

NEAR THREATENED

Cuban Black Hawk

Gavilán Batista (*Buteogallus gundlachi*)
→ Although locally common, this species has a specialized habitat and, consequently, a moderately limited range. Classified as **Near Threatened**. The Red Data Book suggests raising the status to **Threatened** because of its low and fragmented populations where no nucleus has more than 250 mature individuals.

POPULATION ESTIMATE: Fewer than 2,500

POPULATION TREND: Decreasing. Currently the populations have been reduced by 75% from the original potential distribution, which should be in the order of 11,700 sq. miles (30,316 km²).

ESTIMATED AREA: 2,925 sq. miles (7,576 km²)

ENDEMISM LEVEL: Cuba

THREATS: Fragmentation and loss of habitat, deforestation, contamination of water, urbanization (specifically, the construction of hotels and associated infrastructures), and rising sea levels. Specialized wetland habitats have been drained and destroyed. The Black Hawk lives in areas of intense development for tourism; much of its habitat has been destroyed or modified. There is little data on the impact these and other activities associated with tourism have had on the diminishing populations.

CONSERVATION MEASURES ADOPTED: None are known in spite of the fact that about 72% of the range of distribution is located within protected areas with different levels of management.

CONSERVATION MEASURES PROPOSED: Conduct studies to assess population size. Regularly monitor certain sites throughout its range to determine population trends. Monitor trends in destruction of suitable habitat. Protect significant areas of suitable habitat, particularly in the bird's strongholds. Conduct educational campaigns to raise the level of awareness among the local communities that this species does not attack their barnyard fowl.

Plain Pigeon

Torcaza Boba (*Patagioenas inornata*)
This species has a moderately small and fragmented population, and may be declining in some areas. It is classified as **Near Threatened**, but the Red Data Book proposes changing the status of the Cuban populations to **Vulnerable** because of the historical tendency toward a reduction in size from the beginning of the 19th century. Recent studies do not show any signs of recuperation.

POPULATION ESTIMATE: 1,500-6,100

POPULATION TREND: Decreasing

ESTIMATED AREA: 19,382 sq. miles (50,200 km²)

ENDEMISM LEVEL: Greater Antilles

THREATS: The pigeon's preference for coastal areas makes it vulnerable to the destructive effects of severe storms and hurricanes, as well as climate change. Hunting, logging, and clearance for plantation agriculture have reduced populations. Nest predation may affect reproduction in key areas of Puerto Rico.

CONSERVATION MEASURES ADOPTED: A recovery program is underway in Puerto Rico. Conservation efforts are being financed in Cockpit Country, Jamaica. The Plain Pigeon is legally protected in Cuba (but this is not enforced), and has been recorded in several protected areas, including the Guanahacabibes Biosphere Reserve, where it has been the subject of an educational program.

CONSERVATION MEASURES PROPOSED: Survey to assess number and distribution. Assess the impact of illegal hunting. Design captive breeding programs and reintroduce pigeons to areas where they originally existed. Design and implement educational programs to reduce the pressure from hunting.

Cuban Parrot, Rose-throated Parrot, Cuban Amazon

Cotorra (*Amazona leucocephala*)
→ This species is classified as **Near Threatened** because, although not as rare as thought, the overall population is moderately small and continues to decline. It has a limited range, but the populations are not yet severely fragmented or restricted to a few locations. The Red Data Book suggests raising the status of the Cuban Parrot to **Vulnerable** because of the intense and uncontrolled pressure from theft of chicks and consequent destruction of nesting sites.

POPULATION ESTIMATE: Unknown

POPULATION TREND: Decreasing

ESTIMATED AREA: 6,834 sq. miles (17,700 km²)

ENDEMISM LEVEL: Cuba, Bahamas, Grand Cayman, and Cayman Brac.

THREATS: Fragmentation and loss of habitat through natural causes (storms and hurricanes) and anthropic causes continue to be a significant threat. Studies from 1998 to 2008 showed that 90% of nests had been robbed; the remaining 10% were in inaccessible locations. Nest trees are often cut down or cavities enlarged to extract chicks, rendering the nests useless for future breeding attempts. Protective measures are inefficient and the high prices the birds bring on the black market are a strong incentive for illegal activity. Studies conducted in the city of Havana showed that at least 10% of homes posessed Rose-throated Parrots as pets and in some neighborhoods the number reached 30%. Recent monitoring in the field revealed low population density: one bird/sq. mile (0.5 birds/km²) over an area of more than 77 sq. miles (200 km²).

Housing developments threaten the non-breeding habitat of the Abaco, Bahamas population.

CONSERVATION MEASURES ADOPTED: The bird is monitored on Isla de la Juventud and more recently in central Cuba. Artificial nests have been used in Cuba by over 1,300 birds. The species is present in 20 protected areas of Cuba.

CONSERVATION MEASURES PROPOSED: Discourage the theft of birds from the wild through public education campaigns. Encourage better bird-keeping practices to increase longevity of caged birds and reduce demand on wild populations. In Cuba, make and erect more artificial nests. Monitor population trends throughout its range and improve habitat management.

Bee Hummingbird
Zunzuncito (*Mellisuga helenae*)
→ This species is classified as **Near Threatened** because of its moderately small and fragmented population. In spite of the fact that it is fairly widely distributed, the Red Data Book proposes raising its threat status to **Vulnerable** because of the relatively small populations. Studies from 2007 show the abundance of populations in pines and serpentine areas of mountainous zones in eastern Cuba vary between 6 and 10 pairs per sq. mile (2.9-5.2 pairs/km²), while in the arid zone of Guantánamo, the species abundance varies between 6 and 17 pairs per sq. mile (3.2-8.7 pairs/km²).
POPULATION ESTIMATE: Unknown
POPULATION TREND: Decreasing
ESTIMATED AREA: 43,085 sq. miles (109,000 km²)
ENDEMISM LEVEL Cuba
THREATS: The historic decline is principally the result of habitat modification and destruction. Much of Cuba's natural vegetation has been converted to cultivation and pasture for cattle, with only 15-20% of lands remaining in a natural state; the recent expansion of cacao, coffee, and tobacco production poses a further serious threat. The Bee Hummingbird's habitat is fragmented. Its population has diminished 20% in the last 40 years.

CONSERVATION MEASURES ADOPTED: CITES appendix II. It has been noted in 11 protected areas.
CONSERVATION MEASURES PROPOSED: Enforce the protection afforded to the species by protected areas. Discourage further clearing of forests for agriculture. Monitor key populations.

Cuban Solitaire
Ruiseñor (*Myadestes elisabeth*)
→ This species has a moderately small population and occupies a limited range. Classified as **Near Threatened**.
POPULATION ESTIMATE: Unknown
POPULATION TREND: Decreasing
ESTIMATED AREA: 3,282 sq. miles (8,500 km²)
ENDEMISM LEVEL: Cuba
THREATS: Throughout much of its range, forests have been converted to cultivated lands and pasture; there has been a recent expansion of cacao, coffee, and tobacco production. Illegal felling of trees, forest fires, and other catastrophes as a direct or indirect result of illegal hunting are important threats to the populations. The impact of severe storms and hurricanes threatens the survival of the species in some areas. However, habitat in the population stronghold of Pinar del Río province is considered relatively secure.
The Red Data Book suggests changing the status of the Cuban Solitaire to **Vulnerable** because of its limited range of distribution to only two regions, both subject to natural disasters and anthropic events, which could cause severe damage to the populations. Studies done in

2007 showed that in areas of highest abundance, the distribution fluctuated between 0.5 and 1.5 birds per acre (0.38-0.75 birds/hectare).

CONSERVATION MEASURES ADOPTED: None is known. It is found in 10 protected areas.

CONSERVATION MEASURES PROPOSED: Protect forests in the Solitaire's stronghold of Pinar del Río province and its eastern mountain populations. Discourage the conversion of native forests to cash crops. Monitor the population. Conduct studies on reproduction habits of the species.

Palm Crow

Cao Ronco (*Corvus palmarum*)
→ The conservation of the species seems to be deteriorating. Classified as **Near Threatened**.

POPULATION ESTIMATE: Unknown
POPULATION TREND: Decreasing
ESTIMATED AREA: 33,668 sq. miles (87,200 km²)
ENDEMISM LEVEL: Cuba, Hispaniola
THREATS: The reasons for its reduction are unknown, but may be related to competition with the Cuban Crow (*Corvus nasicus*), because habitat alteration has favored the overlapping (intermingling) of the distribution of these two closely related species.

The Red Data Book suggests raising the status of the Palm Crow in Cuba to **Threatened** because of its reduced and fragmented distribution, which, in Cuba, is less than 38.6 sq. miles (100 km²), and limited to six localities, only one of which is within a protected area.

CONSERVATION MEASURES ADOPTED: Part of the population occurs in La Belén, a protected area close to

Najasa in Camagüey.

CONSERVATION MEASURES PROPOSED: Conduct studies to determine its present population and distribution. Investigate the reasons for its decrease and carry out appropriate conservation actions. Improve studies in areas where new populations have been found such as "La 23", an area located on the outskirts of Trinidad.

Cuban Bullfinch

Negrito (*Melopyrrha nigra*)
→ The only living species of its genus. The Red Data Book lists its populations as **Near Threatened** because of the limited geographic distribution range of the species. Habitat is fragmented and diminishing, with an estimated habitat loss of 20% over the last 40 years. Some authors suggest that the Cuban populations could differ at the specific level from those of Grand Cayman, although there is uncertainty about the taxonomic status of both populations.

POPULATION ESTIMATE: Unknown
POPULATION TREND IN CUBA: Decreasing
ESTIMATED AREA IN CUBA: Unknown
ENDEMISM LEVEL: Cuba, Grand Cayman
THREATS: Limited distribution range accounts for considerable impact on the populations from any disturbance, even more so because of the specific differences in the populations.

The main cause for the reduction of populations is the illegal capture for pets, nationally and internationally. The Bullfinch has an exquisite song and this has created a local tradition of songbird competitions that often have high monetary stakes. The impact on the wild populations is unknown, but in the medium and long term, there will be a critical reduction in the size of the population, especially considering the fragmentation of habitats from deforestation, development, tourism, fires, and hurricanes.

CONSERVATION METHODS ADOPTED:
None known. In spite of the fact the bird is found in 17 protected areas, there is no control over illegal song-bird hunting.

CONSERVATION METHODS PROPOSED:
Develop environmental education programs in areas where the species is present. Enforce Cuban laws on the environment; raise and collect fines. Train park staff, forest rangers, and Interior Ministry personnel about the application of the laws and penalties for infractions against the environment and biodiversity.

Conduct programs on the control of illegal hunting in protected areas. Improve habitat management and population monitoring. Perform taxonomic studies to determine the status of the Cuban populations. Maintain control on the Customs aspect of illegal traffic of protected flora and fauna.

Cuban Laws on Conservation

Articles from Cuban Ordinance 200, relating to the applicable legal ordinances affecting people and institutions that could damage in any way the biological diversity of Cuba, within or outside of protected areas. "Species" and "biological diversity" refer to flora and fauna (including birds).

ORDINANCE 200: FINES FOR OFFENSES AGAINST THE ENVIRONMENT (OFFICIAL GAZETTE OF THE REPUBLIC OF CUBA, Ordinary Edition, Havana, Thursday, December, 1999, Twenty-third Year, XCVII, Number 83, Page 1339)

Article 8: It is considered a violation of the laws regarding biological diversity and a fine will be imposed for each incident:
a) Damage or destruction of species of special interest or object of specific protection: 250-5,000 pesos;
b) Collection of flora and fauna without authorization from the competent institutions: 250-2,250 pesos;
c) Violation of the established regulations for the export of species subject to special rules: 250-5,000 pesos; and
d) Trespassing on restricted areas without corresponding authorization: 250-5,000 pesos.

Maps
& Indices

Cuban Tody
(*Todus multicolor*)

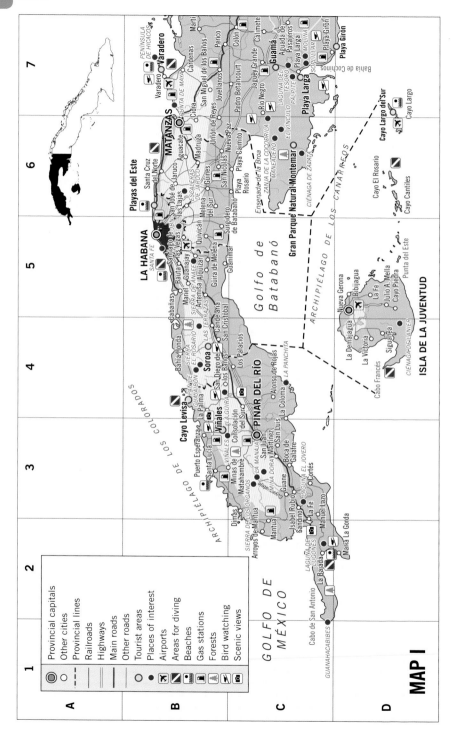

MAP I

Legend:
- Provincial capitals
- Other cities
- Provincial lines
- Railroads
- Highways
- Main roads
- Other roads
- Tourist areas
- Places of interest
- Airports
- Areas for diving
- Beaches
- Gas stations
- Forests
- Bird watching
- Scenic views

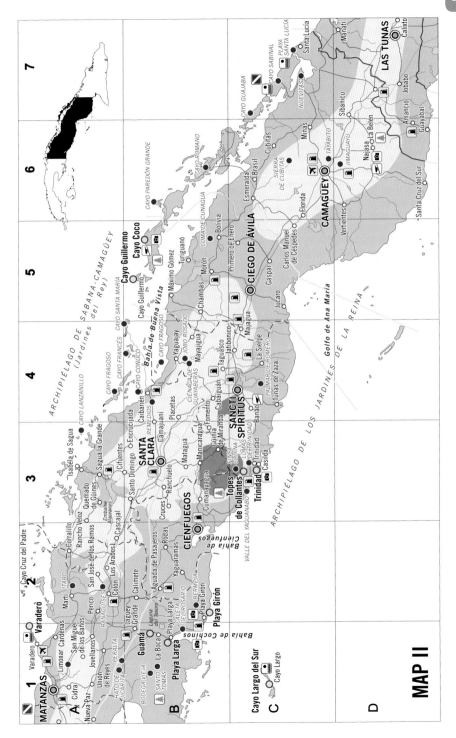

MAP II

149

MAP III

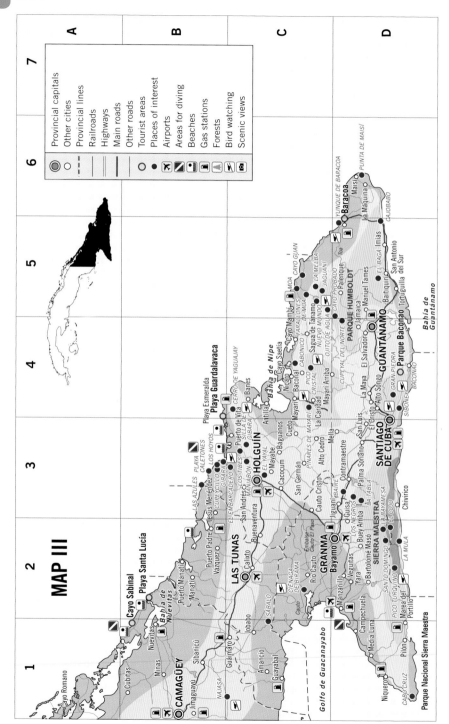

Provincial capitals
Other cities
Provincial lines
Railroads
Highways
Main roads
Other roads
Tourist areas
Places of interest
Airports
Areas for diving
Beaches
Gas stations
Forests
Bird watching
Scenic views

INDEX OF LOCALITIES

Index of Species

Notes

Notes

Notes

Important Dates

Species _____. Date _____
___ Migration ___ Mating ___ Nesting ___ Hatching. Other: _____
___JAN ___FEB ___MAR ___APR ___MAY ___JUN ___JUL ___AUG ___SEP ___OCT ___NOV ___DEC

Species _____. Date _____
___ Migration ___ Mating ___ Nesting ___ Hatching. Other: _____
___JAN ___FEB ___MAR ___APR ___MAY ___JUN ___JUL ___AUG ___SEP ___OCT ___NOV ___DEC

Species _____. Date _____
___ Migration ___ Mating ___ Nesting ___ Hatching. Other: _____
___JAN ___FEB ___MAR ___APR ___MAY ___JUN ___JUL ___AUG ___SEP ___OCT ___NOV ___DEC

Species _____. Date _____
___ Migration ___ Mating ___ Nesting ___ Hatching. Other: _____
___JAN ___FEB ___MAR ___APR ___MAY ___JUN ___JUL ___AUG ___SEP ___OCT ___NOV ___DEC

Species _____. Date _____
___ Migration ___ Mating ___ Nesting ___ Hatching. Other: _____
___JAN ___FEB ___MAR ___APR ___MAY ___JUN ___JUL ___AUG ___SEP ___OCT ___NOV ___DEC

Species _____. Date _____
___ Migration ___ Mating ___ Nesting ___ Hatching. Other: _____
___JAN ___FEB ___MAR ___APR ___MAY ___JUN ___JUL ___AUG ___SEP ___OCT ___NOV ___DEC

Species _____. Date _____
___ Migration ___ Mating ___ Nesting ___ Hatching. Other: _____
___JAN ___FEB ___MAR ___APR ___MAY ___JUN ___JUL ___AUG ___SEP ___OCT ___NOV ___DEC

Species _____. Date _____
___ Migration ___ Mating ___ Nesting ___ Hatching. Other: _____
___JAN ___FEB ___MAR ___APR ___MAY ___JUN ___JUL ___AUG ___SEP ___OCT ___NOV ___DEC

Species _____. Date _____

___ Migration ___ Mating ___ Nesting ___ Hatching. Other: _____

___JAN ___FEB ___MAR ___APR ___MAY ___JUN ___JUL ___AUG ___SEP ___OCT ___NOV ___DEC

Species _____. Date _____

___ Migration ___ Mating ___ Nesting ___ Hatching. Other: _____

___JAN ___FEB ___MAR ___APR ___MAY ___JUN ___JUL ___AUG ___SEP ___OCT ___NOV ___DEC

Species _____. Date _____

___ Migration ___ Mating ___ Nesting ___ Hatching. Other: _____

___JAN ___FEB ___MAR ___APR ___MAY ___JUN ___JUL ___AUG ___SEP ___OCT ___NOV ___DEC

Species _____. Date _____

___ Migration ___ Mating ___ Nesting ___ Hatching. Other: _____

___JAN ___FEB ___MAR ___APR ___MAY ___JUN ___JUL ___AUG ___SEP ___OCT ___NOV ___DEC

Species _____. Date _____

___ Migration ___ Mating ___ Nesting ___ Hatching. Other: _____

___JAN ___FEB ___MAR ___APR ___MAY ___JUN ___JUL ___AUG ___SEP ___OCT ___NOV ___DEC

Species _____. Date _____

___ Migration ___ Mating ___ Nesting ___ Hatching. Other: _____

___JAN ___FEB ___MAR ___APR ___MAY ___JUN ___JUL ___AUG ___SEP ___OCT ___NOV ___DEC

Species _____. Date _____

___ Migration ___ Mating ___ Nesting ___ Hatching. Other: _____

___JAN ___FEB ___MAR ___APR ___MAY ___JUN ___JUL ___AUG ___SEP ___OCT ___NOV ___DEC

Species _____. Date _____

___ Migration ___ Mating ___ Nesting ___ Hatching. Other: _____

___JAN ___FEB ___MAR ___APR ___MAY ___JUN ___JUL ___AUG ___SEP ___OCT ___NOV ___DEC

Contacts

Name _____
Telephone _____
Cell _____
E-mail _____
Address _____
_____
_____
_____

Name _____
Telephone _____
Cell _____
E-mail _____
Address _____
_____
_____
_____

Name _____
Telephone _____
Cell _____
E-mail _____
Address _____
_____
_____
_____

Name _____
Telephone _____
Cell _____
E-mail _____
Address _____
_____
_____
_____

Name _____
Telephone _____
Cell _____
E-mail _____
Address _____
_____
_____
_____

Name _____
Telephone _____
Cell _____
E-mail _____
Address _____
_____
_____
_____

Name _____
Telephone _____
Cell _____
E-mail _____
Address _____
_____
_____
_____

Name _____
Telephone _____
Cell _____
E-mail _____
Address _____
_____
_____
_____

Checklist of Cuban and other West Indian endemic birds
residing in the Cuban archipelago

Family
English name, Cuban name(s) Scientific name, Endemic Family***; Endemic Genus **; **Cuban Endemics** [in bold].

FAMILY: Anatidae
- [ ] 1. West Indian Whistling-Duck/ Yaguasa (*Dendrocygna arborea*)

FAMILY: Accipitridae
- [ ] **2. Cuban Kite/Gavilán Caguarero (*Chondrohierax wilsonii*)**
- [ ] **3. Gundlach's Hawk/Gavilán Colilargo (*Accipiter gundlachi*)**
- [ ] **4. Cuban Black Hawk/Gavilán Batista (*Buteogallus gundlachi*)**

FAMILY: Rallidae
- [ ] **5. Zapata Rail/Gallinuela de Santo Tomás (*Cyanolimnas cerverai*)****

FAMILY: Columbidae
- [ ] 6. Plain Pigeon/Torcaza Boba (*Patagioenas inornata*)
- [ ] **7. Blue-headed Quail-Dove/ Paloma Perdiz (*Starnoenas cyanocephala*)****
- [ ] **8. Gray-fronted Quail-Dove/ Camao (*Geotrygon caniceps*)**

FAMILY: Cuculidae
- [ ] 9. Great Lizard-Cuckoo/Arriero (*Coccyzus merlini*)

FAMILY: Strigidae
- [ ] **10. Bare-legged Owl/Sijú Cotunto (*Margarobyas lawrencii*)****
- [ ] **11. Cuban Pygmy Owl/Sijú Platanero (*Glaucidium siju*)**

FAMILY: Caprimulgidae
- [ ] **12. Cuban Nightjar/Guabairo (*Antrostomus cubanensis*)**

FAMILY: Apodidae
- [ ] 13. Antillean Palm Swift/Vencejito de Palma (*Tachornis phoenicobia*)

FAMILY: Trochilidae
- [ ] 14. Cuban Emerald/Zunzún (*Chlorostilbon ricordii*)
- [ ] **15. Bee Hummingbird/ Zunzuncito (*Mellisuga helenae*)**

FAMILY: Trogonidae
- [ ] **16. Cuban Trogon/Tocororo (*Priotelus temnurus*)**

FAMILY: Todidae
- [ ] **17. Cuban Tody/Cartacuba (*Todus multicolor*)**

FAMILY: Picidae
- [ ] 18. West Indian Woodpecker/ Carpintero Jabado (*Melanerpes superciliaris*)
- [ ] **19. Cuban Green Woodpecker/ Carpintero Verde (*Xiphidiopicus percussus*)****
- [ ] **20. Fernadina's Flicker/ Carpintero Churroso (*Colaptes fernandinae*)****

FAMILIA: Psittacidae
- [ ] **21. Cuban Parakeet/Catey (*Psittacara euops*)**
- [ ] 22. Cuban Parrot, Rose-throated Parrot, Cuban Amazon/Cotorra (*Amazona leucocephala*)

FAMILY: Tyrannidae

☐ 23. Cuban Pewee/Bobito Chico (*Contopus caribaeus*)

☐ 24. La Sagra's Flycatcher/Bobito Grande (*Myiarchus sagrae*)

☐ 25. Loggerhead Kingbird/ Pitirre Guatíbere (*Tyrannus caudifasciatus*)

☐ 26. Giant Kingbird/Pitirre Real (*Tyrannus cubensis*)

FAMILY: Vireonidae

☐ 27. Thick-billed Vireo/Vireo de Bahamas (*Vireo crassirostris*)

☐ **28. Cuban Vireo/Juan Chiví Ojón (*Vireo gundlachi*)**

FAMILY: Corvidae

☐ 29. Cuban Crow/Cao Montero (*Corvus nasicus*)

☐ 30. Palm Crow/Cao Pinalero (*Corvus palmarum*)

FAMILY: Troglodytidae

☐ **31. Zapata Wren/Ferminia (*Ferminia cerverai*) ****

FAMILY: Polioptilidae

☐ **32. Cuban Gnatcatcher/ Sinsontillo (*Polioptila lembeyei*)**

FAMILY: Turdidae

☐ **33. Cuban Solitaire/Ruiseñor (*Myadestes elisabeth*)**

☐ 34. Red-legged Thrush/Zorzal Real (*Turdus plumbeus*)

FAMILY: Mimidae

☐ 35. Bahama Mockingbird/Sinsonte Prieto (*Mimus gundlachi*)

FAMILY: Passerelidae

☐ **36. Cuban Sparrow or Zapata Sparrow/Cabrerito de la Ciénaga (*Torreornis inexpectata*) ****

FAMILY: Spindalidae

☐ 37. Western Spindalis/Cabrero (*Spindalis zena*)

FAMILY: Teretistridae***

☐ **38. Yellow-headed Warbler/Chillina (*Teretistris fernandinae*) ****

☐ **39. Oriente Warbler/Pechero (*Teretistris fornsi*) ****

FAMILY: Parulidae

☐ 40. Olive-capped Warbler/Bijirita del Pinar (*Sethophaga pityophila*)

FAMILY: Icteridae

☐ **41. Cuban Oriole/Solibio (*Icterus melanopsis*)**

☐ **42. Red-shouldered Blackbird/ Mayito de Ciénaga (*Agelaius assimilis*)**

☐ 43. Tawny-shouldered Blackbird/ Mayito (*Agelaius humeralis*)

☐ **44. Cuban Blackbird/Totí (*Dives atroviolaceus*)**

☐ 45. Greater Antillean Grackle/ Chichinguaco (*Quiscalus niger*)

FAMILY: Thraupidae

☐ 46. Cuban Bullfinch/Negrito (*Melopyrrha nigra*)

☐ **47. Cuban Grassquit/Tomeguín del Pinar (*Tiaris canorus*)**